DELIVERED:
TRUE STORIES IN PIZZA DELIVERY

Josh Walker

ALSO AVAILABLE FROM THE AUTHOR:

Luke Coles and the Flower of Chiloe
Luke Coles and the Forest Assassin
Luke Coles and the Curse of Corpo Seco
Luke Coles and the Army of Cesares
Caleuche Chronicles
Luke Coles Anthology
Shadowed Dreams
Phoenix Dawn and the Rise of the Witch
Mission Memories
Monster Attack

COMING SOON:

Knights of Pegasus
Chilote Folklore
Delivered 2: True Stories in Missionary Work

Delivered: True Stories in Pizza Delivery

Printed in the U.S.A. and Great Britain

1st edition

For more information see
www.joshwalkerbooks.com

ISBN: 978-1-944621-26-1

**LIBRARY OF CONGRESS NUMBER:
2020912873**

FORGOTTEN PLACES
PUBLISHING

Josh Walker

Table of Contents

Josh Walker

To all my pizza delivery co-workers, past and present. Thank you for the experiences and the inspiration.

Josh Walker

FIRST DAY

When I accepted a job delivering pizza, I didn't know what to expect. In part, I thought delivery drivers sat around waiting to take deliveries. I figured they messed around on their cellphones, shot the breeze, so on and so forth. At the beginning of my first shift, I noticed that wasn't the case.

While I stood by the restaurant's office, I watched the other drivers. They hurried from one part of the store to the next, mixing casual conversation with some strange code. "Yeah, my daughter got an A on her test. Does anyone have a tag for a fourteen-piece wings? She graduates in two months. This address looks familiar. What should I do for her graduation party? Did they want mango-hab?"

My co-workers carried out a plethora of tasks. They folded boxes, answered phones, applied stickers to the boxes, and moved trays of dough from the walk-in to the makeline. They took those dough balls, slapping them into pizzas, did dishes, pulled pizzas from the oven, swept the floor, cleaned countertops, and of course, took deliveries out to their cars. How did they know when to do what? Did they have assigned tasks? Was a manager coordinating? More important...how would I know when to do what? How could I learn without slowing down the others?

"Videos are ready." The manager on shift called out, exiting the office and using his thumb to point over his shoulder. "When you finish, there will be a multiple-choice quiz. After the quiz, watch the next video and take its quiz. Keep going until all the videos are over."

I nodded, shuffled past him, and sat in a small office space. It was large enough for two people at most. Then I turned to the computer and clicked play. The videos explained the different stations in the store.

They went over safety and health regulations. They explained pizza store terminology, expectations, how to make food, and store policies. One video described how my blood was pizza sauce. If it wasn't before, it is now. I've eaten a lot of pizza over the last five years.

The information from the videos was a lot. What I learned from observing the store was also a lot. Both of those things together were overwhelming. I didn't absorb it all at once, but I set a goal. I'd learn a new skill each shift and reach the minimum level of proficiency therein. How could I prioritize those things? Was it more important to know how to make a pizza or be able to pull one out of the oven and slice it? Was it more important to understand how to apply the stickers—I learned they were called tags—on boxes or know how to fold a box? Was it more important to know how to answer phones or help a carryout customer? I'm still not sure I know the answer to any of those things, but I have learned to do them all. Now, I'm the co-worker moving mindless from one task to another, saying, "N means pineapple. Did you see the movie last night? K means bacon."

After video training, the manager did a car inspection, assuring my car was safe, registered, and insured. Then he partnered me with another driver who would be my trainer for the evening. I rode with my trainer on two or three deliveries. He showed me how to use the driver tag for each order to identify if the delivery was a cash or card payment.

He demonstrated how to use the tags to track tips and how to use the computer system's map. He taught me how to organize the extra items and drinks that came attached to each order. When returning from each delivery, I learned how to drop card slips and cash into my box. Then he rode with me during two deliveries. Once he felt I was ready, I was on my own.

Aside from the aforementioned, I learned a lot during the first week. Here's a list of ten things you might not know about delivery drivers.

1. During the last two hours when a restaurant is open—the last hour especially—drivers work on a list of cleaning tasks. They must complete this list before they can go home. When a restaurant closes at

midnight, it isn't uncommon for the drivers to get out at 2:00 AM or even later. If you order during these times, you extend the driver's shift. When it takes them ten minutes to get to your house and back, their night becomes ten minutes longer. If they get an average tip or better, they don't mind this.

2. In-store, drivers make anywhere from minimum wage up to $15.00 an hour.

3. When in the store, drivers make more than while on a delivery. Depending on the company, when drivers leave the store, they make anything from $2.00 an hour up to minimum wage. With most places, its around $4.00-$4.50 an hour.

4. Tips while driving vary in an unpredictable manner. Sure, specific neighborhoods tip more. Younger age groups seem less aware that they are supposed to tip. This is by no fault of their own; in simple terms, they haven't learned yet. They don't know any better.

5. The average tip is four and a half to six dollars. Though, a ten-dollar tip is common.

6. About one in twenty people don't tip.

7. During a workday, there are busier times: the lunch rush, the dinner rush, and on occasion, a late rush. If an evening seems slow, drivers will get sent home. If a store is low on drivers, and a sudden rush hits, a driver's shift can extend by hours.

8. At rush, drivers can take anywhere from two to four deliveries an hour. In large part, this depends on the distance traveled while on each delivery.

9. When two orders come in at the same time, both going to the same neighborhood, the orders get sent out at the same time. To speed things up, they go with a single driver.

10. Pizza delivery is a dangerous job. According to most studies, it is among the top five most vulnerable in the United States. More on this later.

I understand this is a lot of information to take in. By no means was I able to learn all the above in one day, nor one week, nor one year. After five years, I continue to learn new things. Every day provides a unique experience, an original tale, a new lesson from a customer.

With the above context, I want to share some of my most memorable encounters with you. I've wanted to do this for a while. But I've been working on my high fantasy novel, homeschooling my kids during the COVID-19 pandemic, and working delivery shifts. It hasn't left me with much free time.

In the accounts that follow, I've changed the customer names and identifying details to protect their privacy. But these stories and the messages behind them remain true to my memory...maybe with some embellishment. I hope you find them as memorable to read about as they were to live through.

FIRST DELIVERY

Doing something for the first time is awkward. When you do it by yourself, without anyone else's help, the strangeness of it amplifies. You never know what to expect. Such is the case when you go from learner's permit to driver's license. In that situation, the emotional scope of the experience changes. The license represents new levels of independence.

In those circumstances, a person might forget something. Did they position their rearview mirror before they started to drive? Did they take off the parking brake? Is the car in drive? Reverse? Is the seat in the correct position?

When on a delivery by myself for the first time, I went through my own mental checklist. Did I have the driver's tag? Was it a credit card delivery? Did I have the credit card slip? Were there any extras, things like marinara sauce cups and the like? Were there any drinks? Is the bag secure on my seat? Did I know where I was going? After running through those essential questions, I began toward a neighborhood called Sun Valley.

Under normal circumstances, the drive takes five to seven minutes. It depends on the traffic. As a driver, the company policy is to drive three miles under the speed limit. As such, driving there while on a delivery would take longer.

Yet, that first delivery seemed to take forever. It was a warmer afternoon, and my air conditioning was slow to cool the car. But regardless of temperature, I would have been sweating bullets. I could feel my anxiety building, bringing with it an element of lightheadedness. To remain calm, I didn't even have the radio on; I had to focus.

Once I entered the neighborhood, I kept an eye out for the street. When it came up, I made a left turn. Then I began to scan the numbers of the houses. This proved more difficult than I'd realized. I had to navigate the curving road—cars parked on both sides—watching for traffic, and scanning houses. Later, I would learn about google maps, and finding homes would become much more manageable. Yet, this was my first delivery. I was Red 5, not yet a Jedi Master of pizza delivery.

The house numbers indicated I was close to the delivery, each house bringing me closer. Three houses to go. Two. Then, anxiety building, I arrived. My hand shook, moving the shifter into neutral before pulling on the parking brake. Should I open the passenger side door and grab the pizza bag that way? Should I lift the bag and slide it out the driver's side door with me? I chose the latter, lifting the bag with both hands, rotating it over the steering wheel and out the door. With caution, I swung my legs out of the car, planting my feet firm against the ground and standing.

Don't pass out. Don't pass out. Don't pass out. I repeated in my mind, transferring the pizza bag to my right hand and shutting the car door with my left. *I'm sure the customer will be nice. You didn't forget anything.* Step by step, I walked up the wide, concrete driveway—it shone a bright white under the sun—and I reached the front door. Tunnel vision got the best of me, so I don't remember if there was a porch or not. I don't even remember the color of the house. White…I think?

I rang the doorbell, waited two seconds, and then I remembered the credit card receipt. It was still in my pocket. My thoughts began to race. *Can I get it out before the customer an-swered?* I have to try, right? Maybe I shouldn't try? *Maybe I should wait until they answer and pull it out in front of them? Would it be rude to put my hand in my pocket in front of them? Oh, no! I hear them on the other side of the door.*

After all this, something interesting oc-curred; I've always considered it a good omen. A friend from high school answered the door. She wasn't someone who I spent time with outside of school. Aside from speech and debate, I don't remember having many classes with her. Yet, she was someone who I always appreciated and respected, the kind of person who projects kind-ness. It was like she wanted the people around her to feel comfortable. Her ability to fulfill that want came with a natural effortlessness.

From high school, I remembered conversations about Playstation 2. She was a fan of Resident Evil. I recalled one time when we made Quesadillas in debate class. We had a shared appreciation of Buffy the Vampire Slayer. From social media, I knew she'd become a college-level English teacher and a copywriter. She also made a short film where she beats up zombies. It's a fun watch.

Upon recognizing me, she offered a smile, "hi, how are you?"

Instead of answering immediately, I remained stuck on the credit card receipt. *Was it still in my pocket?* It was. *I'd have to get it after. Wait…did she say hi? I should say hi back.* "I'm good. How are you?" *Good, that didn't come out as awkward. You're an expert delivery driver. Keep it up. Wait…give her the food.* I began to hand her the food. "How is work?"

"Good," she took the pizza, "I've been busy grading essays, needed a food break."

"Cool," I nodded. *Did I give her the receipt yet? I sure didn't.* I reached into my pocket, removed it, and held it out to her. At that moment, I realized my pre-delivery checklist failed me. I held the receipt up to her, horrified to make eye contact, admitting with sheepish embarrassment, "I forgot a pen."

"No problem, I've got one. I'll be right back." She retreated into the house, returning half a minute later, a signed receipt and pen in hand. She held them out to me. "You can keep the pen."

"Thanks," I took the pen and receipt, saying. "have a great evening."

"You, too." She closed the door as I turned and began back toward my car.

First delivery down, thousands to go.

Josh Walker

CO-WORKERS

At any given moment, the restaurant has around thirty employees. The majority are drivers. Three to five are managers. Five to seven are insiders. The insiders tend to be high school and college students. Their primary responsibility is to make the food.

When I did social work, my co-workers had college degrees and professional experience. When I left that field, I didn't expect pizza delivery to provide me co-workers who seemed as intelligent, if not more so, than my social work co-workers. But pizza delivery provided just that.

The talents of the people who work in the restaurant are incredible. If I wrote this book without including a brief description of these people, I would be remiss.

As such, I want to dedicate this section of the book to my more memorable co-workers. To respect their privacy, I gave them nicknames. I should also note that I left out some. In large part, this is because I'm not sure how happy some would be to appear in a book, even if I didn't use their name.

Dungeon Master was one of my first co-workers. He was an insider who loved Dungeons and Dragons, Star Trek, Comics, so on and so forth. As these are many of the things that interested me, we bonded over them. He took an interest in writing. Since I am an author, I tried to mentor him in this interest. Shortly after he left the restaurant, he left for college at the University of Wyoming. There he continued to write D&D scenarios as a Dungeon Master. One of his campaigns—one involving a half Soulflayer—gained national popularity. He's become a regular beta reader for my novels.

Ladies' Man was the driver who first took me out on deliveries, teaching me the basics of pizza delivery. Many of the female drivers, and one of the insiders, admitted to having crushes on him. Having served a short term in the military, he'd retired young. During the time when we worked together, he was studying at the local community college. He reminded me that it's okay to relax and enjoy life.

Princess was Princess's actual nickname. He was one of the first co-workers I met, and for me, he was a helpful teacher. Last I heard, he drove a shuttle for a local car dealership.

Hard Worker was a driver who worked my first opening shift with me. She may be the fastest, hardest worker I've ever been around. In one hour, she seemed to be able to finish what I've come to learn is three to four hours' worth of work. She never slowed, never had to stop to think. Everything was instinctual for her, and she made prep work look easy. She is currently a manager at one of the other stores. I've tried to imitate her fast, smart work.

Retro Gamer was a driver. His day job involved substitute teaching for the school district, usually for P.E. classes. He enjoyed playing retro video games, especially Tecmo Super Bowl. Growing up, it was one of my favorite games, too. He helped me remember the joy of childhood, a time where video games made the world go round.

Movie Fan is Retro Gamer's brother. Like his brother, he was also a driver. Both enjoyed video games. Yet, Movie Fan expressed more interest in popular movies and television shows. He had a particular affinity for superhero films. He had once been a manager but preferred driving over running shifts. Like his brother, he helped me remember my past filled with superhero cartoons.

Realist was a driver who always kept things real. He treated everyone with respect and was one of the co-workers who showed up at my book signings. He even traveled to Denver for a signing, almost two hours away from Cheyenne. Where he proved supportive in most things, he is upfront with his thoughts. When he has issues with people, he speaks to them and resolves those problems. One time, we talked at length about a series of books we wanted to write together. It led to my writing Shadowed Dreams. The possibility exists that we make it into a series which we co-author. He moved away, and recently, become a first-time father.

Daredevil loved cars and practical jokes. He started as an insider, and at 18, switched to become a driver. If you heard an airhorn going off in the store, you knew he was the cause. If you heard a car without a muffler, it was also him. Whenever I had car trouble, I could go to him for suggestions about how to fix it. He even helped me repair some smaller issues. He lived life like it was a race, feeding on the adrenaline it provided him. He was eager to learn, asking questions of everyone around him—it didn't matter what the topic—and absorbing all he could from their answers. Unfortunately, he died at a young age. I'll always remember him for having one of the most prominent personalities I've encountered.

Star Valley is a manager from Star Valley, the same area of the state where my mom grew up. When closing the store, Star Valley worked to get out early. It was a trait I appreciated because she often helped with closing tasks. Corporate gave her a new store, making her the General Manager. Shortly after, she found a regular boyfriend, settled down, got married, and had a child. It's been a true joy seeing the pride she takes in motherhood.

Well-Rounded was the manager who interviewed me before I started at Pizza Place. I learned right away that he enjoyed video games, Eve Online being the one he mentioned as one of his favorites. He has played bass and guitar for a plethora of bands.

According to my memory, his current band is Alpha-A. They are worth looking up on Facebook. Well Rounded tended to have informed opinions about most topics: politics, movies, pop culture, or gaming. It didn't matter what came up, he was able to contribute to the conversation.

Psychologist was a manager who seemed to understand everyone around him. It was a trait that made him supernaturally personable. He understands what bothers people. He knows what cheers them up, what keeps them feeling comfortable. He's excellent at giving advice and never shies away from a joke. His personality and work netted him his own store where he is now a General Manager.

Storyteller is the General Manager of the store where I work. The positive attitude he holds toward people and his desire to bond with them competes with his need to be a boss. It is a balancing game to him, and he has learned it well. In life, people experience countless adventures. He's already faced enough for three lifetimes, and he has a talent for recounting them. In the end, he's loyal to a fault, putting his family and friends first.

Party Girl was a manager. She demonstrates an insatiable external joy for life. When there is a celebration, she is at its center. She's often the one who helps people break out of their shell. While she doesn't show it to many people, she sometimes lets slip that her life is not all rainbows and sprinkles. This is what makes her ability to cheer others such a unique talent. It's why she's earned the respect of so many of her co-workers.

Crazy Cat Girl is Party Girl's best friend. She's got enough attitude for both of them...and she loves cats. Where she demonstrates an external hardness, her love for her daughter shows a softer side. She started at Pizza Place shortly after me, and we closed the store together for years. As such, I can say that once she's picked up a task, she nails it down, perfects it, and learns to do it as fast and precise as anyone.

Quarterback was a manager and former high school quarterback. This went well with my love for running routes and catching footballs. When the weather allowed, we tried to go to work early and play some catch before our shifts. He left the store for a different pizza place before settling on a career as a plumber. Less than a year back, he helped me replace a broken water heater in my basement. When I say he helped, I mean he did it for me.

Favorite Insider was one of the insiders when I started. He was so efficient at doing all aspects of the insider work, including some of the managerial duties, that we nicknamed him the Favorite Insider. He transitioned to being a driver. Then he went to college. Even so, he still works with us between semesters.

Welder is an insider who loves music and cars. He keeps it real with those around them, not willing to pander to anyone, but still staying respectful. While he continues to work in the restaurant, he's training to be a welder.

Youtube is a singer with many other creative aspirations. She's a writer, an actress, a dreamer, a philosopher, and someone who won't settle for less than her best. With her friends, she is a great judge of character, always willing to go the extra mile to help them.

Marine is a retired marine and current marathon runner. In terms of the restaurant, he's been a driver my whole time in the store. He tries to remain well-rounded, participating in multiple extra-curricular activities. He does Tae Kwon Do, takes college classes, participates in a church band, and does anything else he can find to occupy his time. When he has a home improvement project, car trouble, or other major life events, he is quick to talk about it. I've learned how to do a lot of things from him. And I've heard plenty of stories about his time in the military.

Music Editor is an insider and high school student. Where we share many movie and video game interests, he has a passion for music. His Instagram shows how his love and talent translate to some pretty cool tracks. On those tracks, he plays most of the instruments, adding overlays and editing songs together.

Artistic Hippie seems like she was born in the wrong era. She is a true artist at heart, and by all physical appearances, a hippie. She was a driver when I began working with her. Since then, she's moved on to sell home and car insurance. If you live in Cheyenne, ask me about how to contact her for a quote. Though she changed jobs, we've kept in touch. Within the last year, we began to work on co-producing a comic. Oh, and she loves plants.

Pre-Med began work as an insider weeks after I started as a driver. Her strength was in how she related to those around her. Her rarest talent is the ability to learn about the passions of others. When she left Pizza Place, she began studying microbiology.

Sweetheart isn't a nickname I give to this co-worker. Her father—a cop—pulled me over one night. I'm convinced he pulled me over because it was late, there was no other traffic, and he wanted to meet one of his daughter's co-workers. He immediately brought up how his daughter drives for our store. I asked, "who is your daughter?" When he said her name, I couldn't help but smile, explaining, "everyone in the store loves her." That's when he described her as a sweetheart, hence her name in this book. She's a hard worker who shows a genuine interest in the wellbeing of others. Once school starts up, again, she plans to work toward becoming an ultrasound tech.

Deku is one of the managers and a huge anime fan. By his name, you might be able to guess his favorite anime. Aside from anime, he enjoys football, movies, and video games. Where he started as an insider, he's gone from that to running shifts to Assistant Store Manager. If he is working or participating in a hobby, he has a certain meticulosity to everything he does. As a result, every small detail he touches has a polish. Generally, he has a relaxed demeanor but has shown a decisive edge in the completion of his work duties. I have also known him to purchase longboards on impulse.

Reign is Deku's roommate and another manager in the store. He earns his nickname from his love for Reign creamsicle energy drinks. Once, he asked me to get him one from a gas station. By accident, I got him Rainbow Unicorn Bang. Oops. He has a level head and a maturity beyond his years with how he perceives his surroundings. In most situations where people stress, he stays calm, working his way through it. It's a demeanor I've always appreciated.

Reign's Brother is Reign's younger brother. I could also call him the tallest teenager I've ever met. He's a down to earth insider who is hyperaware of his sur-roundings. His observations allow him to make friends with everyone around him. With ease, he learns the skills he needs to circumvent every situa-tion in which he finds himself.

Mr. Chill is one of the drivers. He's worked for the restaurant for as long as I have. He sells fireworks by day, working rush shifts with us in the restaurant. The nickname defines him. I've never met someone who has a higher capacity to roll with the blows which life deals him. A rock accident caused him to suffer foot pain. It got so bad that he chose to have the foot amputated. Shortly after, he invited many of us to a funeral for his foot.

Politician is a driver who closes with me with a regular frequency. He ran for public office at one point, earning him his nickname in this book. When he finds interest in a topic—usually one with a focus on health, pop culture, or politics—he does his best to learn about it. He is a huge Star Trek fan who always holds to his convictions.

European Historian is another driver who closes with me. He loves reading and pop culture. We've had some good conversations about Brandon Sanderson's novels. When the topic of college came up, he explained he has a degree that involves European history. I can't remember what he said the degree was in, though. If I had to guess, I'd say medieval history.

Outdoors earns her name from some pictures of a hunting trip she shared with her dad. Shortly after me, she started as a driver, but she had been an insider before. As such, many people in the store knew her. Her abilities as a single mom impressed me, how she balanced the work and home life. She later moved on to work for a bank, got married, and became a mother to a second child. When at work, she kept up a high energy, creating a fun work environment.

Tokyo Ghoul is Outdoors's sister. She is an anime fan who loves to party. Tokyo Ghoul seemed to be her favorite anime, but we talked about a few. We also talked about a few books we've both read. At current, she works as a manager at another pizza store. She recently shared a funny story on social media where her lawn guy hit on her. I'm not sure if there was a point to that...but the way she handled it and shared it with us was hilarious. In short, she needs a new lawn guy. Anyone know a good lawn guy?

The Hunter was an insider when I started. He loved talking about guns, camping, fishing, and the out-doors. Injuries seem to plague him. Before he'd graduated high school, he'd already gone through a significant shoulder operation. Even so, he never backed down from doing a handstand or demonstrat-ing some strange pushup. He transitioned into the role of a driver before joining the military. An injury at basic training has forced him to transition to civilian life. He attended Eastern Wyoming College where he learned about gunsmithing.

Swag is an insider who teaches me all the phrases that cool kids use nowadays. I can then implement said phraseology in my books. She has a personable charisma which makes it easy for everyone get along with her. When at work, she hurries to get her job done. And when she gets a chance, she helps others finish their work, too.

No Sleep is an insider who used to be a manager at another store. She enjoys playing video games and watching anime. One time we discussed "No Sleep" stories. They are scary stories that people write, putting them online under the premise that they might be genuine. A person can read them on Reddit or listen to them on youtube. For me, anyone who likes those types of stories gains instant trust.

Other Author is one of my friends who is an author with the same publisher. In the past, he has been a gun store owner, a member of the military, an appliance salesman, and he had his first book published before I started elementary school. At current, he also owns a used video game, magic cards, and Warhammer store. He continues to love guns and once gifted me an AR-15 for Christmas.

Kiki is a practicing Wiccan and an anime fan. I combined those two things to come up with her nickname. Anime fans will understand why. She is a hard worker who works opening and closing shifts, filling in where she is needed. She is a fan of the video game series Kingdom Hearts. That same series is what my wife played to learn English. As such, Kiki and I have plenty to talk about.

Cowboys Fan is a manager from another store who fills in at my store. He is Kiki's significant other. They recently moved into a home together. We like many of the same video games and are both avid fans of the NFL. Unfortunately, he likes the wrong team.

IN THE COLD

In 1869, Major General Grenville Dodge founded Cheyenne. I like to think he reached the Rocky Mountains and gazed upon the majestic purple and green, snow-capped peaks. Then, after short contemplation, he said, "nope, I'm not going over that." At that point, he stopped in place and established what would become Wyoming's capital. The location makes the town vulnerable to winds from the northwest. They come as a gale, accelerating down the mountains.

During the winter, that wind magnifies the dry cold of the region. In those conditions, snowflakes become daggers of ice against exposed skin. On colder days, I've felt the hairs in my nose freeze, and my muscles tighten. The skin turns red and numb. Shallow breathing expels visible puffs of air.

At one in the morning, the cold magnifies. If I'm working a driving shift in those conditions, I use layers under my uniform. I don't want to have to take a coat off whenever I return to the store only to put it on for the next delivery. That takes too much time. I'd prefer to use every free second to work toward the close, toward going home at the end of the night.

Once the car warms up, it becomes easy to stay warm. Even so, every second out in the cold hurts the exposed skin on my face.

The worst cold comes when I get to a house, ring the doorbell, and have to wait. I worry the doorbell might not work, so after twenty seconds of waiting, I knock. After another twenty seconds, no one comes to the door. As such, I struggle against the wind: keeping the pizza bag balanced, pinning the receipt with the person's phone number down, and using numb fingers to pull my phone from my pocket. If I can achieve that, dialing the number becomes the next challenge.

Once the call goes through, they answer, "hello?"

"Hi-i-i-i-i," my voice trembles as I shiver in the cold, "thi-i-i-i-s is J-o-o-sh from the p-i-i-i-z-a-a pl-a-a-ce. I'm he-e-e-e-re."

"Oh," they act surprised. "I'll be right there."

Two minutes later they answer the door, "sorry about that, I had to toss on some pajamas. I was downstairs playing video games."

On the inside, I berate them. *If you aren't going to wait for it, why order food? It isn't like it's a surprise that I'm here. Do you always play video games in your underwear? Like is that a thing? Have I been playing video games wrong my whole life?*

On the outside, I say, "no worries," complete the transaction, and retreat to the warmth of my vehicle.

Last winter, I had one of those deliveries which had me waiting in the cold for several minutes. After this, I returned to the store. I checked to see if we'd received any other deliveries. We hadn't. Then I checked the hour. It was closing time; I wouldn't take any more deliveries that night. I let out a sigh of relief.

An hour later, I finished the dishes and moved to the front of the store to help the other closing driver. That night, the other closing driver was the Marine. As we worked, we talked about things: movies, politics, and the like. Due to the loud hum of the fans over the pizza oven, we had to speak louder than we usually would.

But we reached a point in the night where we could turn them off. No sooner had we done this than we heard a hollow tap, tap, tap, against the glass at the front of the store. We both snapped our heads up, staring in the direction of the sound.

Sometimes—after we've closed—people come to the store, asking if we're open. When we explain we've closed, we get different reactions. Most people understand and return to their cars. Others try to negotiate. They don't realize it will take time for the oven to heat up. Then we'll have to pull the toppings and dough from the walk-in, so on and so forth. Not to mention the fact that we would have to rewash and resanitize everything. All that could add another 45 minutes to our night. A rare few of these people lash out at us. They call us lazy for not doing our jobs, declaring that the internet says we're open—it doesn't—insisting that we do what they want.

Keep in mind, we don't open the door to these people. We either yell through the glass, have them call the store, use paper and pen to write notes back and forth, or play charades. "Are you saying you're a hippopotamus? That doesn't make sense. Oh, I get it now! You've closed the store. Okay, bye."

One time, I saw a man—wearing a hoodie and mask before the COVID-19 crisis—park along the curb in front of the store. As if he were a contestant on the Greatest Race, he leaped from his car, rushed up to the door, and pulled. It was locked and didn't move, so he hurried back to his car and sped off. For some reason, I doubt he had good intentions. Then again, he could have needed to use a restroom.

On that cold night—the one when Marine and I both snapped our heads to the sound of tapping on the glass front door—there stood a woman. She was around twenty years old, wearing torn jeans and a t-shirt. She had no coat, no hat, no scarf. In the cold night, her skin had turned a bright red, and she shivered. In a way, the manner in which she shook seemed violent. We wondered how long she might have been there, unheard, her taps drowned out by the oven fans.

As I looked at the woman, it reminded me of a few years earlier. A local high school girl had crashed her car. After, she wandered to her high school a few blocks away from the accident. There she died from exposure near an entrance to the school.

I knew Wyoming's cold could be deadly, and the woman who I saw through the glass was in real, immediate danger.

Even so, we knew we needed to be careful. At night, it wouldn't be beyond a potential robber to use a woman as bait so they could get into the store. With the jeans and t-shirt she had on, it was easy to see she didn't have anywhere to hide a weapon. She, by herself, would pose no threat to us.

While Marine went to the store manager to get a key to the front door, I went to the door itself. From there, I got a better look at the woman's face. Her eyes were wide with tears forming in them; her brow furrowed; her frowning lips twitched. She's afraid, I realized.

I shouted through the glass, "my coworker went to get a key."

With that, she nodded her understanding, but the fear remained in her expression.

From my position at the door, I glanced left and right, taking in the whole of the parking lot. Aside from a white sedan in the far corner, well over two football fields away, I couldn't see anything. There were no other cars, no other people, nothing, only the woman and the cold.

Marine returned with the key and opened the door, inviting her to come in and sit down.

"Thank you," she stepped past him in a hurry, but she didn't sit down. Instead, she asked, "can I please use your phone?"

"That's fine." We told her, asking. "Is there anything we can help you with? What were you doing out there?"

"My boyfriend...I guess he is my ex-boyfriend, now...we were at the grocery store. The store was already closed, so we couldn't go in. Then we got in an argument. He broke my phone and drove off without me." She held up a smartphone.

I've seen scratched and broken screens before, but I've never seen a phone in this condition. The phone bent at an angle, the screen shattered to a point where pieces of it had fallen out. The interior electronics of the phone were visible through the broken screen. "I need to call my mom. She can come to get me. Crap, I can't believe this. Mom told me not to move in with this guy. Now, I don't even have a home anymore. I hope my mom lets me go back home."

We showed her where the phone was, and she called her mom. There was no answer.

What was strange to me was how the woman remembered other phone numbers, too. I haven't memorized someone's number since high school. I struggle to remember my own half the time. Yet, this woman called three other people, one after another.

As she made these calls, Marine and I got together. If she were not able to contact someone, we came up with a plan. It involved one of us driving her wherever she asked us to take her. The other one would follow behind to keep an eye on the situation.

It was a contingency we didn't have to carry out because, on her third call, someone answered. Though I didn't hear the other end of the conversation, from the woman's side, it went like this, "yeah, I know it's been a while. I'm at the Pizza Place. Can you come get me? ... I know it's been a long time... I know ... I'm sorry about that... Please, I have no one else... Thank you... Yeah, I'll watch for you."

Twenty minutes later, a red truck pulled into the parking lot in front of the store. We unlocked the door, let her out, and watched her jump into the passenger seat of the truck.

I never heard any follow up to this, don't know what became of the woman. Even so, during that cold Wyoming night, I'm glad we were in a position to help her.

YOU WILL NOT MUG ME, KID

The intersection of Taft and 14th street is the location of my most memorable delivery. Where many of the stories in this book have happy endings, or moral messages, or a light feeling, this one does not. It is dark, and it still bothers me to this day. I'm not sure I'll ever get over it, and I considered not including it in this collection. Yet, I don't think this anthology would be complete without it.

There is a home near this intersection which rents out its basement as an apartment. From the intersection, it is easier to reach this house than from any other area. One night, I received an order to the upstairs address. Upon parking on the corner, I noticed two kids, middle school-aged, half a block south of me. As I got out of my car, I saw the pair of kids pick up speed. Often, kids do this to make a joke. "Hey, I ordered that. Hahaha."

Instead of waiting for them, I made my way to the door and knocked. The man who answered the door informed me, "I didn't order it; it must be the bottom apartment."

"I bet you're right," I agreed. After all, the bottom apartment ordered a lot. "Sorry to bother you so late."

"No problem." He closed the door.

41

At this point, I noticed the middle school kids had stopped near my car. They appeared to be waiting for me; I heard one of them warn the other, "you shouldn't do this."

Are they going to ask for a ride? I wondered. *They might hit me up for a few dollars.* It wouldn't have been the first time it happened. Whatever they wanted, I decided it could wait for after I made the delivery to the back apartment.

Before I could begin toward the back of the house, I heard a voice shout from my car. "Give me your pizza." The kid disguised his voice, trying to make it raspy. Where he wanted to sound like Christian Bale's Batman, he came off like an old lady who had smoked too many cigarettes.

I chose not to acknowledge him, taking two steps toward the side of the house, hoping the kids would be gone by the time I got back.

"Give me your pizza, or I shoot." This time he emphasized the word shoot, extending the vowel sound, still with an old lady voice.

I stopped mid-stride, turned around, and sure enough, the kid was holding a black, semi-automatic pistol, pointing it at me. Federal law requires toy guns must have a blazing orange tip to show they aren't real. The weapon this kid held didn't boast said orange tip.

I immediately thought about my kids—I had two at the time. The third wasn't conceived yet—and I thought about my wife. If something happened to me, I hoped they'd be okay. If all the kid wanted was pizza, I could do that. But the way he held the gun, the malice in his eye, his disregard for me up to that point...it all told me there was more to this than pizza. It was about power. He wanted to establish dominance over someone; he sought to control them, make them afraid. With that type of callousness, he could take the pizza and shoot me anyway.

Then a strange thought came to me. Why disguise your voice but not hide your face? I will always remember his face: young like a baby, blonde hair, blue eyes. At that time of night, he should have been at home, not pointing a gun at a stranger. Didn't he realize the impact his actions could have? On his life, mine, my family's, his family's, even his friend's.

I kept an eye on his friend. He stood ten feet away with wide, scared eyes. Even he couldn't believe what his friend was doing.

My family returned to my mind; memories of them stirred emotions. The strongest of those sentiments was sadness. I didn't want my time with them cut short. Knowing I didn't have much time to react, I pushed thoughts and emotions from my mind and went into survival mode.

First, I gauged the distance between the kid and me. I'm not confident he could have hit me if I took off running at an angle and then zigzagged back behind the house. But my phone was in the

car, and I wasn't sure I'd be able to find someone to help me call the police at 11:00 PM. Plus,
there was always the chance he got a lucky
shot. It wasn't a sure thing I'd escape unscathed.

"What?" I signaled to my ear, acting like I
didn't see the weapon, pretending I had a hear-
ing problem and stepping nearer to him. The distance between us shrank to ten feet.

"Give me your pizza!" He demanded a third
time, moving toward me and lifting the gun to
make sure I saw it.

I pretended there was no gun, shifting the
bag to my left hand. With caution, I slid toward
him, acting confused until two feet separated us,
"I can't hear well. What are you saying?"

He lifted the gun, shaking it in my face with
the barrel pointed up at the sky. "Give me
your…"

I dropped the pizza bag, snatching his wrist
before he could point the gun back down at me. I
rotated to the side: straightening his arm, push-
ing my forearm against his elbow, spinning him
off balance, planting his face into the ground.

Throughout this action, I felt the gun go off;
its projectile sped by me to my right. But no
sound accompanied the shot, and the gun didn't
recoil. The slide didn't rack back before returning
to its place. I left the boy sprawled out on the
ground, taking the gun and standing. All the
while, he swore at me and rolled around, "you

broke my nose. It's a toy. You broke my nose. It was a joke."

I didn't need to examine the weapon to confirm his claim of it being a toy. Lightweight plastic gave it away as fake. Heck, the way the projectile shot—whatever it was—proved the gun wasn't real. I pushed a button near the grip and pulled the magazine out. Airsoft pellets. Did I break this kid's nose because of airsoft pellets? Was I afraid for my family's wellbeing because of airsoft pellets?

I sighed, shunting away anger and asking the kid, "Do you want me to call your parents or an ambulance?"

He answered with a string of swear words before standing and lunging for his airsoft gun. By reflex, I pulled it away. As strange as it sounds, it relieved me to see his elbow worked. If I'd wanted, I knew I could have broken it, but controlling the weapon was enough. I didn't want to break the elbow. Even so, his nose seemed a bit crooked.

With another sigh, I handed the gun back to him, repeating my question. "Do you want me to call your parents first or an ambulance to check out your nose?"

He answered with another slew of swear words and took off down 14th street. After a slight hesitation, his friend followed.

I picked up the pizza bag and checked the pizza. It survived the drop. Good thing it was hand-tossed; a thin crust would have turned into a jigsaw puzzle. When I delivered to the basement, the person who answered tipped two dollars. If they knew I fought off a gunman to save their pizza, would they have tipped more?

After completing the delivery, I pulled out my phone, calling the police. In case the kid got home and spun a story for his parents, I wanted the police to know what happened. It kept my bases covered. After rehashing the story to the police, I explained I didn't want to press charges or anything. The kid's nose had already paid the price for his poor decision. Still, I asked them to get a hold of me if they discovered anything.

The officer explained, "Chances are he won't tell his parents what happened. He understands that you called us, so he'll make up some story to stay out of trouble. He'll say he tripped and fell, anything to keep us from getting involved. He won't want his parents talking to us."

As I mull over that night, I contemplate what I could have changed. If I thought giving the kid the pizza would have solved the situation without violence, I would have done it. I wouldn't have even hesitated. If he asked for the pizza and my car keys, I'd have done that, too. If I thought running was the best option, I would have done that. Yet, my own safety was my priority. And for some reason, I felt moving close to him and taking the weapon away was my best chance.

In a weird way, it's comforting to know that were it a real gun, the bullet wouldn't have found me. Even so, I do have some dark sentiments associated with that night: distress, anxiety, and the like. I never wanted to hurt a young teenager. Nor did I want to ponder what would happen to my family without me. It isn't a situation anyone should ever be in.

In the end, I hope the kid learned from the experience, never trying something so careless, again.

Josh Walker

CAR TROUBLE

When you drive for a living, your car goes through a lot. When you spend half the year driving in the snow, those problems amplify. While in my first year of pizza delivery, I drove a 2013 Dodge Dart. I bought it new, and at around 4,000 miles, began using it for delivery. That's when the trouble started. Within the first two months, the CD player went out. A few months later, the passenger side automatic window stopped working.

To me, these weren't significant issues. I didn't care, so long as the car drove. Not to mention, I loved the car. The True Blue Pearl Color held a unique brilliance, a dark shade with flecks of silver. When a bright, midday sky shone against the car's sporty curves, the blue became reflective. It was a more transparent color in which a person could see the clouds.

One night, the store manager asked me to go to one of the other stores. I can't remember what he needed. It could have been five or six bags of some topping, more likely a few trays of dough. I hopped in my Dart and began toward the other store. The route took me through the only two-lane roundabout in town. When it comes to that roundabout, there are three kinds of people:

1. The people who think they are competing in the Cheyenne 500 Grand Prix. They speed up before reaching the circle, and after they pass through it, they keep their speed up. It provides them a strange adrenaline rush and an unhealthy amount of competitive hostility toward those with whom they share the road.

2. Then there are the people who are hesitant to use the roundabout. To them, it represents a change in a growing town. It means learning new rules, accepting that things aren't as simple as they used to be.

and

3. Those who shrug and continue as usual.

On the way back to my store—pizza dough…or it could have been pizza toppings…in my back seat—I pushed in the clutch on my Dart. The stick moved from first to second gear, and I heard a pop. The car lurched and decelerated: grinding to a stop, whining, and leaving me stranded at a two-lane entrance to the roundabout. I'd driven cars with a bad clutch before, so I knew what to look for, signs to indicate a clutch was wearing. I had noticed no such signs, so I didn't think the clutch was bad. I wondered, is it the transmission? *If so, at least the warranty covers it. After all, the car only has 12,067 miles.*

I pushed the clutch to the floor, using a

soft hand to manipulate the shifter, testing out first gear. Instead of slipping into place, smoke began to spew from the hood. I sighed, left the stick in neutral, turned off the car, and pulled the hand lever to engage the parking brake. Then I turned on blinkers and pulled out my cell phone, calling my store to send another driver to help me. With their help, one of us could push the car while the other steered it into a nearby parking lot. As it was, I wouldn't be able to push and steer by myself. I'd have to wait in the car for his arrival.

All the while, the anger in the Cheyenne 500 drivers built. Some flipped me off as they zipped around me.

The people adverse to change seemed more annoyed, having to adapt to a new circumstance. They offered me lecturing glares. How dare I stop in the middle of the road.

The third kind of people tendered understanding shrugs and empathetic nods. People behind me began to merge into the lane on the right, making their way into the roundabout.

Before my co-worker arrived, a patrol car pulled up behind me, and two officers got out. I rolled down my window, explaining my situation, and they offered to push. Once the car was out of the way of traffic, resting in the parking lot, I thanked them. Then I called a tow truck to come to get the car. The officers chose to wait with me. I'm not sure if they didn't have anywhere else to be, wanted to rest after having pushed the car, or didn't trust me to not try to take the vehicle back onto the road. It might have been a combination of all those things. Either way, I knew the car wouldn't go anywhere on its own, at least not until it got repaired. As such, they didn't need to worry about me moving it.

The tow truck and my co-worker arrived at the same time. The truck took my car to the dealership, and my friend took me back to the store. I cashed out my money and clocked out, catching a ride home with Quarterback. Once we arrived at my house, he stayed, and we played some Tecmo Super Bowl and that year's version of Madden.

It helped me relax and keep my mind off the car. It also helped me introduce my daughter to the 1989-1990 49er roster. Since then, we've watched lots of classic football games together: the game where Jerry Rice broke Jim Brown's touchdown record, the game where Derrick Thomas got seven sacks in one game, and the game where Bo Jackson ran over Bosworth on the goal line.

She became a fan of the 90's 49ers team as well as the current team; her favorite player is George Kittle. She likes how he runs over people and says funny stuff. But I digress.

The next day, I heard back from the dealership. The disc in the clutch had burned out, fragmented, and sent debris into the starter, fly-wheel, and shifter assembly. The mechanic had to replace it all. The dealership explained that because the clutch was a wear part, it wasn't covered beyond 12,000 miles. Remember. My car had 12,067 miles. I was 67 miles beyond the warranty.

These are the worst situations for a driver. We earn our money by driving, and without a car, we can't make money. Without money, we can't fix the car, and the repairs that time were around $6,000.00. It's not a fun place to be, but before too long, the car was back on the road.

12,300 miles later—when the car was at 24,367 miles—the clutch burned out, again. That time, only the clutch assembly needed replacing. At 50,000 miles, the clutch began to go out. That time, I could feel it going, the sponginess of it. At that point, I traded the Dart for a 2013 Chevy Malibu LT. The Malibu has been a much more stable—albeit less sporty—vehicle. Aside from a blown coolant overflow tank and some charging issues, it gave me a solid three years.

Then, about a year back, my sister got married. Due to a long drive on the highway with her 2003 Honda CRV, she noticed it was losing oil. At which point, she and her husband decided it was time for them to get a new vehicle. I inherited that Honda. I thought it would be helpful on snowy days, and it would provide me a second vehicle for when my Malibu was in the shop. After six months, the Honda became my primary delivery vehicle. As with the Malibu, the Honda requires little in the way of maintenance. Yet, that doesn't mean I haven't had my adventures with it.

For example, on the way to work, I was at the same two-laned roundabout. A person in the roundabout slid up over the median and crashed into me. The Honda held up with nothing more than a dented door, not even enough to cause problems with the door opening.

Aside from repair issues, the snow has proved another challenge to me. I can't count the number of times I've had to use a snow shovel to dig myself out. One of those times, it was two in the morning; I was on the way home after a shift. Another time, while on the way to a delivery, I got stuck three times.

Though, as far as being stuck in the snow goes, one experience stands out to me.

The manager assigned me to take two separate deliveries to a neighborhood on the other side of town. The drive was at least twenty minutes, the fastest way there a rural backroad. The trouble I faced was deciding which delivery to prioritize. They had both been waiting over thirty minutes. It would be another twenty before I made it to them. And there was another problem. The deliveries appeared close on the map, but they weren't connected by residential roads. I'd have to exit the neighborhood and loop around to reach the second delivery. Regardless of which address I went to first, this would be the situation.

As I planned a route, I loaded the pizza's in my car. Then I crawled my Honda toward the first house. Along the way, I stopped at two separate cars that had gone off the road, flashers blinking. No one was in either, so I continued to the assigned houses. After the first delivery, my GPS pointed me to the second, suggesting I take a road I'd never seen before. A sign was up for it, indicating a street was there.

Though I didn't see any tire tracks to show as much. I sighed. Instead of looping around, I decided to chance going up the side street. About 2/3 of the way there, my car got stuck. Even the Honda's all-wheel-drive couldn't save me. I called the customer, explaining my situation, telling him I was going to walk his food the three remaining blocks. I figured I'd come back and take care of my car after the delivery.

He kept asking questions, so I couldn't hang up and begin toward his place. It felt like I was a serial killer, and he was a detective trying to track our call. Something was up, but I couldn't tell what. Then a Dodge Ram 3500 pulled up ahead of me, stopped, and a man climbed out. Three others followed him, one from each of the truck's four doors. I stuffed my phone in my pocket and jumped out to meet them.

The passenger explained he was the one on the phone, how they saw me get stuck. By the time I'd called them, they were already on their way to help. We attached a chain to my Honda and to their truck.

As we worked, we talked about Wyoming, its weather, and its people. Like me, all four had spent most of their lives in the state. They liked hunting, fishing, and the outdoors. Those are more my dad and sibling's cups of tea, but I know enough about the topics that I can hold a conversation.

One of the men explained he was studying at the University of Wyoming, working on a degree in English. He aspired to become an author.

I explained to him that I am an author, giving him one of my cards, offering to help him with writing and publishing. In short, I could show him the ropes. He took it, and we've kept in touch. He's a fantastic writer, as talented as some of the best I've come across. He recently graduated, accepting a teaching job at a rural, Wyoming High School.

One of the men took the pizza from me, paid for it, and ate in the truck while we worked to get me out. It made sense. With too many of us working on digging and getting the chain on my car, we would only get in each other's way.

Once free from the snowtrap, I said good-bye to the four and returned to the store. The man who ordered the pizza has continued to order from us at least once a week. Every time I deliver to him, he gives me a $13.75 tip, apologizing for the snow incident. After, he catches me up on all the news involving his friends.

I explain it wasn't his fault, and I appreciated his help.

I wish I could think of a deeper theme for these stories.

The theme could be that people be understanding of one another. Things aren't easy for people. Even when you don't know the semantics of the job another person does, appreciate that they do. Respect the sacrifices they make.

So maybe a theme might be gratitude? I will always be grateful to that truck full of fellow Wyomingites.

In truth, I submit the purpose of this chapter, and of this book, is to show the adventure that is life. Every day we live through experiences worthy of any Hallmark Christmas scene. Of course, we should appreciate the friendship which those escapades earn us. We should remember the kindnesses we encounter. During the stress of harrowing challenge, we must find joy in our own narratives. Life will never be perfect, but that's part of what makes it fun.

TIPS: THE GOOD, THE BAD, THE UGLY

Tips are essential to delivery drivers. Often, not always, we gauge how much we like a customer by how much they tip. As such, in many of the stories in this collection, I mention the significant tip amounts which regular customers give us.

As we appreciate these high tippers, we also remember every customer who never tips. When we see their address pop up, it makes us hang our heads and sigh. If we get two or three non-tippers on the same night—not common, but it happens—it can ruin our mood for the whole week.

This chapter will focus on some of the most memorable tippers and non-tippers across whom I've come.

I want to start with some of those who never tip. I don't do this to complain. Instead, I want to contrast, differentiating the bad experiences from the good. After all, that's what life is about, withstanding the bad moments to magnify the good ones.

But before I get into the stories, I wanted to go into some of the reasons why people don't tip. Included with the reasons are my answers to them.

1. REASON: I only have money for the food, not for the tip.

REPLY: If your budget is this tight, consider saving money by driving to the store. There you can take advantage of one of the better carryout deals. Plus, you won't get the delivery charge—which doesn't go to the driver—and that will save you another $2-$5.

Also, if your budget is that tight, ask yourself this. Is eating out the best idea in the first place? If you decide to order food, include the tip in your consideration. Plan for it and make it an automatic thing. When you order, tip.

2. REASON: I don't believe in tipping. Corporations should pay their employees a fair wage for the work they do. It isn't my job, as a customer, to pay their employees for them.

REPLY: This is a fair opinion, and I won't argue with it. Yet if you believe this, I need to ask. Have you contacted the company, expressing your views on this, letting them know how you feel? Call them. Explain to them how you'd prefer to have the employee's wages included in the cost of the food. It will raise the price of everything on the menu, but you won't have to worry about tipping, anymore.

Make sure that if you don't tip on principle, because you feel it is the company's job to pay the employees, that you are working to make the systemic change. Don't let the drivers become the victims of your self-righteousness.

3. REASON: They don't tip in Japan. They don't tip in Australia. They don't tip in England. They don't tip in wherever else I have traveled. The variant of this is, "I'm from Germany. We don't tip there."

REPLY: You're in a different country where tipping is necessary. The employee wages are not included in the food prices to the same extent as they are in your country. Some drivers count on your tip to be able to buy their child a new backpack for school or a new coat for winter. The $4.50 base pay they make will not be enough to take care of the immediate necessities they may have.

4. REASON: I don't tip because I'm teaching the driver a lesson. Not tipping shows them how if they want to earn more, they need to go to college, get an education, and get a real job.

REPLY: Aside from being condescending, this bases itself on a faulty premise. The majority of the drivers drive as a side job. They come in for the rush, working for one to three hours for two or three nights a week. Many of them are military. Some are in school. Others are retired and work to supplement their retirement income.

I remember one situation where I delivered a pizza to a girl at the local chain bookstore. I had recently done a signing at the store, but the girl was not one of the workers present at the signing.

She gave me the usual, "I don't tip as a favor to motivate you to do better," line.

I shrugged it off and handed her the food, commenting on the book she was reading. It was one of mine, <u>Luke Coles and the Flower of Chiloe</u>. I talked to her about it, asking her thoughts about specific characters and scenarios. She explained how the book reminded her of Harry Potter. She told me she loved the characters and the accurate folklore, elaborating on some of the deeper themes within the text.

After the passage of two or three minutes, she asked me how I knew so much about the book. I smiled, saying, "well, I wrote it."

After her condescension, she couldn't help but turn a bright red, and that was tip enough.

In short, don't assume anything about people. Especially, don't assume things about people based on their hobbies or employment. You never know who they are, where they've been, or what's their story.

5. REASON: The most common explanation of why people don't tip is that they don't know any better. Where I see this is in high school kids, people who are ordering food for the first time. My guess is it is kids who have money from their first job. It is exciting for them to order food for the first time.

REPLY: Parents, teach your children to tip.

With that, I'm going to move into some stories which involve memorable tippers and non-tippers.

We have a regular customer who orders late at night, usually paying with cash. They live in an awkward dead end that is easy to get to, but difficult to leave. It is along the busiest road in town, across from a home improvement store. The intersection boasts a stoplight, but at night, that light is stuck on red. One time, I waited fifteen minutes for it to change; it didn't.

So to leave that delivery, I have to turn right, going away from my store before looping back around. It turns what would be a 5 minute delivery into a 10-15 minute one.

The person who orders pays exact change. Was the total $15.84? If it was, he gave me a ten, a five, three quarters, a nickel, and four pennies. Sometimes, he even pays a little less. Though, I don't think he does that intending to short the driver; rather, it's an oversight. Even so, one night, I counted the money before he closed the door. I never took it out of my hand, showing it to him, "the total was $16.19. You only gave me $16.00."

He answered with a cocky smile, "it's only nineteen cents. Are you so stingy that you are going to make me round up nineteen cents?"

I smiled back, nodding, "I get paid $4.50 an hour, and anything I am short, comes out of my tip money at the end of the night. I can't be responsible for paying for your food."

He grumbled something, pulling a bill from his pocket and handing it to me, "here's a dollar. Keep the change. Apparently, you need it."

That was the only time I ever got a tip from him. He continues to order, giving exact change to pay. Though he hasn't shorted me since.

Speaking of people who try to short me money. There was another regular, late-night customer who would pay with bags of coins. The first time I delivered to him, I got back to the store, counted the money, and realized he was five dollars short. The next time I delivered to him, I explained I needed to add the money in front of him. With a sheepish reluctance, he agreed, and I counted. He was ten dollars short; he grumbled and paid with bills.

The next time I delivered to him, when he saw it was me, he swore aloud. "Are you going to count it again?"

I shook my head yes.

He dropped the bag of coins on a counter next to him and paid with bills.

From that point on, he continued to pay with bills instead of coins.

Again, I don't tell these stories to complain. It is all about contrasting the bad experiences with the good ones. In life, there are deeply unpleasant times. This is true in every walk of life. We need to be able to brush those off. At the same time, we should strive to not be an obstacle in the lives of other people. In other words, we should focus on the good around us and be the good around others.

Now, I want to go into some of my favorite experiences involving tips. I'd considered giving these their own chapter, but they are shorter stories. They are one-time encounters, lasting a few seconds. I don't think I could stretch them out beyond half a page.

The first of these involves a girl, no older than seven or eight, with blonde hair and pigtails. She answered the door, handing me thirty dollars on a fifteen-dollar order. I went to give her change, and she replied, "it is my birthday money. I bought pizza for my family, and daddy says I should tip to be nice, so I want you to have the tip."

I wished her a happy birthday. The next day, I sent a copy of one of my books to the family, twenty dollars, and a note inside the cover. The message that I wrote on the note explained I'd recently come across their family, but they wouldn't remember when. It told them that because they impressed me so much with a random act of kindness that I wanted to return the favor. I explained the twenty dollars was a late birthday present to their daughter, adding the book was a present to the family. I signed the book with the inscription, "Here's to random acts of kindness."

This next experience is the most recent one. It happened last week. I'd already finished this chapter, but I needed to include what happened in this book.

Thirty minutes before close, we received a delivery. The instructions attached to the order read, *guys I'm so sorry I know ya'all are closing and getting ready to go home. I wish I had more to give you.* The order had a thirty-dollar pre-tip attached.

Another story involves a delivery to a hotel on the outskirts of town. On busy—or icy—roads, it is twenty minutes both ways, making for an extended delivery. When I got to the room, the people inside spoke in Spanish, one asking, "¿Debo darle una propina o no?" *Should I give him a tip or not?*

The other responded. "Sip, dale una." *Yeah, give him one.*

"¿Cuanto?" *How much?*

"No sé. Preguntale cuanto quiere." *I don't know. Ask him how much he wants.*

All the while, I stood, not letting them know I understood the conversation, listening as they went back and forth. In the end, they decided to ask me how much I wanted for a tip. Before he could ask, I answered in Spanish, "dame lo que crees que sea justo." *Give me what you feel is fair.*

He laughed, "treinta dolares entonces, so-lo porque hablas Español." *Thirty dollars then, only because you speak Spanish.*

I told him that was too much, but he had already written it on the receipt. To date, it remains among the top four best tips I've ever received.

Another of the four biggest tips involved an older woman who gave me a wad of cash, saying, "keep the change." I got back to the car, counted it, and realized it was over a $30.00 tip on a $12.00 order.

I went back and knocked, thinking she might have made a mistake. Sometimes people confuse a ten-dollar bill for a one.

She yelled through the door, "it wasn't a mistake."

Before I continue with the story about my largest tip ever, I need to explain something. Every now and then, the store receives an order to feed a full football team, fifty people at some church activity, or forty employees at a staff meeting. Those tend to be $200-$300 orders. With those high dollar orders, sometimes the tip is $50 or more. In those cases, we split the tip with the managers and insiders who worked to make the food. As such, I'm not including those among my top four tips.

The most substantial tip I ever received was on an order that came in at midnight. It was in the middle of a snowstorm, on a street where I'd already been stuck that night. Luck was with me on the run, so I got within two blocks of the house without bottoming out. Even so, I knew I wouldn't get closer while driving. Instead, I took the food and walked the rest of the way.

The man had paid for the food with a card. Yet, when I delivered, he handed me three, crisp, twenty-dollar bills. Then he explained. "one is for the snow, another for ordering so late, and the last is the normal tip."

After paying for the food, he turned back to his eight or nine-year-old child—with who he appeared to be watching marvel movies—and the man said. "It is important to appreciate what other people do and show gratitude to them for their time." As a parent, it is an important lesson to teach a child. As adults, it is an important lesson to remember.

OH, DEER

At the beginning of my shift, I prefer runs that take me north and south. They help me avoid the blare of a setting sun, especially during the summer. At that time, sun impaired vision prevents me from seeing the sparrows that chase moths all over the roadways.

After returning from one of those sunset deliveries, I began doing dishes. During a rush, I don't always get a break to work on closing tasks, so it was a nice pause. A full half-hour went by before I heard the manager call, "Josh, you have a delivery to Gettysburg."

"On it," I shouted back, dropping the dish I was washing back into the dish sink filled with soapy water. On the way to pick up my delivery bag, I grabbed a hand towel to dry my hands.

By the time I reached my car, the sun had set. Generally, deliveries are much better after sunset. Aside from no sun to fight with, there is less traffic, I can get from point A to point B that much faster. Yet, on the way back to the store, I ended up with someone behind me who kept their brights on. He followed me down a two-lane road that runs north and south on the east side of town. *Why doesn't he pass me?* I wondered. His lights shined through my back window, making it impossible to give full attention to what was ahead. To mitigate the brightness of his lights, I flipped my rearview mirror down.

At that same second—from the side of the road—out jumped a deer. It landed in front of my car, forcing me to slam on my brakes. As I screeched to a stop, the car behind me moved to the other lane, zipping past me, speeding down the road. He missed the deer by inches. How did he not see the deer with his brights on? The world may never know. After I'd stopped, I stared at the mule deer in front of me. It was a buck; I couldn't tell if three or four points.

After staring at me for a few seconds, the animal looked back toward some bushes. They were near the sidewalk from where he had jumped. Two more deer came out. All three stared at me one more time before continuing across the street.

By the time I returned to the store, the driver of the car behind me had called the store. He claimed I brake checked him, confirming he hadn't seen the deer. I explained what happened to the manager, and we laughed it off, glad an accident hadn't happened.

At that point, another delivery was waiting for me. It took me up a street three blocks west of the one where I'd seen the deer. As I took the order, I drove careful, knowing deer were in the area. About two minutes toward my destination, the buck—this time accompanied by the other two deer—ran in front of me.

Alertness gave me plenty of time to react,

so I stopped, letting them get out of the road. As the buck went by, he seemed to glare at me. It was like he was saying, "Stop trying to hit me. I'm on to you now. If this happens, again, there will be trouble."

I waited until the deer disappeared into a neighborhood to the west. Then I took my foot off the brake and pushed in the gas.

The rest of my shift proved uneventful and slow. We were out of the store by 12:30 AM. It's always nice to be back home before one. It signifies I'll get a solid six or seven hours of sleep before I have to wake up, take my wife to her job, and then go into dad mode for the day.

On the way home, about a block away from my house, the mule deer buck jumped in front of me, again. For the third time, I had to slam on my brakes. This time, I missed hitting him by inches. He grunted at me, tapping his horn against my hood. Okay, he didn't really tap his horn. But he did glare at me. Was he jumping in front of me on purpose? Did I have a deer stalker?

He waited for the other two deer to follow him before they turned into a neighborhood—my neighborhood—and ran down *my* street.

I gave them a few minutes to get some distance before I continued home. I didn't want that deer to know where I live.

RETURNING HOME

After a closing shift, sometimes I make a trip to a 24-hour Walmart. It's on the way home, so I don't have to go out of my way to get a Gatorade, washer fluid, cereal, or something else I might need. At night, Walmart is more comfortable to navigate. There are no lines and no crowds. The ambiance offers a nice cool down as I get back into an at-home mindset.

Almost exactly four years ago, from the time of my writing this, in July, a week before Cheyenne Frontier Days, I got off work. At that point, I began the drive toward Walmart, knowing I needed some diapers for my three-week-old son. Though, he had half a day worth of them left, so I knew I could have gone in the morning. Even so, I wanted to pick them up and be done with the chore.

As I reached the stoplight that determines if I go to Walmart or go home, I zoned out and turned toward my house. At that point, I felt torn. That specific road has a baseball field where I could pull in. From there, I could loop back to Walmart, and I had every intention of doing it. But then I got a feeling. As a religious person, I'd refer to the feeling as heavenly inspiration. A physics professor might refer to it as a connection to the universe. A practitioner of Shinto might call it a call from their ancestors. Regardless of what you call it, the impulse to return home was tangible, and I knew I had to obey it.

The street where I lived was a one-way, so I had to go one block beyond it, then loop back around. The final turn before reaching my street left me at the top of a hill with my headlights pointing directly at my house.

At the gate of my house, stood a man. I guessed him to be in his late forties or early fifties. He was thin, with weathered skin, and wispy black hair. He wore a large backpack on his back, giving me the impression that he was a vagabond.

When my lights illuminated him, he went from messing with my gate—I thank God every day that it has a trick to opening it—and the man stared at me. He was waiting for me to pass. I am a non-confrontational person, prone to let a disagreement go rather than start a conflict. Though, when I saw this man in front of my house, my initial impulse was to continue straight at him, running him over.

Still, I knew that might be extreme, so I pulled next to the sidewalk, my lights remained pointed at the gate. After a few seconds, he turned back to my gate, trying to open it. At that point, my little bichon, Momo, barked at the man through my open living room window. To reach that high, she had to stand atop my couch, a place she knew she wasn't supposed to be. Yet,

I was grateful she'd disobeyed because each time she barked, the man shied back.

Beyond the couch, I could see my wife, cleaning. I know I'm biased when I say this, but I have a beautiful wife, and that night, she looked as amazing as ever. I hoped my wife would look up and to see why the dog was barking, but she seemed to have in earbuds, so she didn't notice.

I pulled out my cellphone, calling the police and letting them know what was going on, explaining I was going to confront the man. They advised me to wait, but there was no way I'd heed that advice. For that three-minute call, the man continued to try to figure out the gate. He pulled back each time Momo barked.

Once I hung up with the 911, I pulled away from the curb, pointing my headlights straight at the man. I wanted to be able to see him in the dark, so I parked that way in the middle of the road. Then I got out of the car and asked him, "Do you need something?"

He squinted his eyes at me, blinking as they adjusted. Then he forced an unnerving, sinister smile to his face and answered, "I'm here to see Theresa. You don't need to worry about it." I'd expected slurred speech, but he spoke clearly: squaring his shoulders, puffing out his chest, and taking an aggressive step toward me.

At that point, I realized de-escalating the situation would prove difficult. As such, I sized him up. While I did this, he moved his hands inside the pockets of his trench coat. If he had a weapon, I'd be at a disadvantage in a fight. At the same time, I was bigger...and I'd trained in martial arts for twenty years.

My eyes glanced to the window of my house, hoping my wife had noticed us. If she had, she could go grab her rifle...or kitchen knife...or a sword...anything really. If the guy got passed me, I wanted her to have another line of defense. It would also give her a chance to shut and lock the window. She still hadn't seen us, but our dog watched and whined.

My eyes shifted back to the man's worn face. His smile remained, but impatience had snuck into his expression. He wanted me to leave, wanted to scare me away. Finally, I spoke. "No one named Theresa lives here." Healthy anger and righteous indignation fueled my words. It helped me keep up an appearance of authority.

"Sure," he smiled, signaling toward my wife with his head. "That's her right there."

"That's my wife." I glared. "Along with her, my three children are inside that home. Those four people are the most important thing to me in the world, and right now, I see you as a threat to them. You need to go."

He frowned, moving his hand around in his pocket and taking a step toward me. "I thought

Theresa lived here. She looks like Theresa." His voice was monotone, detached, not a hint of emotion in it.

I acted like I was pointing at my wife as I shifted forward, pointing my shoulder at him, shrinking my profile in case he decided to attack. I tried to make the movement casual, so he didn't see it as an act of aggression. Then I told him. "That is my wife, which is why I already called the police. They are on their way. If you don't go, now, you'll be here when they get here. Your choice."

The mention of police caused him to freeze. His eyes pointed up and his head bobbed as he mumbled to himself. After a few tense seconds of this he looked back to me. "I should go. Theresa doesn't live here." Then he sped walked around my car to the other side of the street and continued in the direction of downtown.

When he was out of sight, I returned to my car, moving it from the center of the street to the curb and entering my home.

"Oh," my wife smiled as I opened the door, "you're home. Did you get the diapers?"

I'll always be grateful to the higher power that guided me home that night. And whenever I remember Momo—she passed away unexpectedly this year—I'll remember how she defended our family that night. I don't know how long the man had been there before I arrived home, but Momo wouldn't let him in without a fight.

The moral of the story is that families are essential and that dogs are amazing. Also, dogs are family.

WE DON'T HAVE MOUNTAIN DEW

One summer night, someone called the store. I glanced at the clock, saw it was after midnight, and answered. "Thank you for calling Pizza Place. I'm sorry. we're closed."

"You better not be ******* closed. Thirty minutes ago, I ordered food from you, and you messed it up."

I used their phone number to pull up their order, a single 8-piece wings. The other driver wasn't back from delivering it, yet. Then I check the oven to see if it was still on. It wasn't. The other driver had turned it off. "I'm sorry to hear that. Is..."

"You better bring me more **** wings." She interrupted.

"I'll turn the ovens back on and get those cooking." I'd hoped to compensate them for the meal or give them a free meal the next time they ordered... Though, I wasn't going to argue with them. "It will take us a bit longer than usual to get those wings out to you because our oven will take a few minutes to warm up."

Behind me, I heard the manager click on the oven. He must have been listening to the call.

"It better not take longer." She shouted. "You messed these up. You better fix it."

"I apologize for the mistake." I maintained my composure, asking. "Could I offer you something else for the inconvenience? Something to drink or a dessert?"

"Yeah," she kept an angry tone. "Give me a brownie."

"Yes, ma'am," I told her, explaining, "we'll get the wings and brownie out to you as soon as possible."

I heard the call cut out on her end.

"Ma'am?" I wanted to make sure she wasn't still on the line. When I didn't get an answer, I hung up.

Before I closed out the order, I checked one more thing. The computer tracks how many times we've given a person free food. It turned out this woman had ordered an 8-piece wings the night before and complained three times to get new wings. And that night, she complained twice more. The call I answered was her sixth complaint in two days. She'd already received five orders of wings for the price of one.

I called the manager over to make him aware of it. Then I sent the order through, turned on the oven, and went to the walk-in to pull out the wings and brownie.

Half an hour later, I pulled up to her apartment building. To keep me going that night, I had a twenty-ounce Mountain Dew. I took a quick drink before I grabbed the pizza bag and got out of the car.

The apartment was in one of the complexes where a person has to go inside to find the apartments. In her case, the address was in the three hundreds, meaning the apartment was on the third floor. Coincidentally, I noticed a woman watching me out one of the third-floor windows.

I bet that's the apartment, I thought, beginning toward the building.

After two flights of stairs, I reached the right floor, found the apartment, and knocked. When the woman answered, I saw at least ten adults and a handful of kids inside. "It's about time," she snapped, snatching the box from me before I even had it all the way out of the pizza bag. "We're hungry. The kids haven't even gotten any wings, yet."

As I turned to leave, I forced a smile. "Have a great day. Enjoy the food."

No sooner had I got back to the store than the phone rang. I clocked in from my run and answered, knowing what to expect. With as many people as they had in their apartment, they were going to try to get at least two more free orders of wings. Sure enough, her voice shouted, "our wings weren't cooked enough. Are you stupid there?"

"I'm sorry to hear that." Unfortunately, our ovens have been off for too long. We won't be able to replace your order tonight."

"**** you won't. And the driver forgot our Mountain Dew, too. I saw him drinking it himself, so you have to bring us our drink and an extra one, too."

I explained, forcing agitation from my voice. "We don't carry Pepsi products, so we don't have Mountain Dew."

They asked, "Why did the other person there say you did?"

Annoyance within me built, but I answered with calm resolve. "Ma'am, your order didn't include a drink."

She insisted. "I placed the order online and ordered a Mountain Dew. I see it right here in front of me."

"Didn't you say you talked to someone when you placed your order?" I asked. "I know this is the case because I'm the same person you talked to last time. Ma'am, you might have thought about asking for a drink. Though I assure you didn't mention a drink to me, and it definitely wasn't Mountain Dew."

"You said you don't have Pepsi? So you have Coke?" She grumbled. "Sprite sounds good. You will bring it to us for free, right?"

"No," I told her. "We can't help you with that because you didn't order a drink."

"What about a free pizza? Or you could re-place my wings." She demanded. "You know, for the trouble of not getting our order right."

A free pizza because you are a liar? Also, didn't you hear the ovens are off? I forced the thought from my mind and agreed with her. "Okay, we'll have some wings right out. It will be about an hour because we have to turn the oven back on, and it will take a while to heat up."

If I didn't know she might have hungry kids in the home, I would have left it at this, letting her wait for an order of wings that was never com-ing. I wasn't stupid like she seemed to think; res-taurant workers aren't. They understand when someone is talking down to them, treating them poorly, taking advantage of systems. Letting her wait for something that would not come would have been perfect karma. Yet, I didn't want to leave her kids like that. If they needed to eat, I wanted to help them.

Thirty minutes later, around 1:30 AM at that point, we'd finished closing the restaurant. I called my friend Luis, the owner of a 24-hour Mexican place down the street, asking if he could make wings. He said he could, so I ex-plained the situation, placing an order of 40 wings with him. Since he was the owner, he charged me the wholesale rate on the 40 wings.

After retrieving the wings, I returned to the woman's home, still in my Pizza Place uniform, and knocked.

"About time..." she began shouting but stopped once she realized I wasn't holding my usual pizza bag.

"Ma'am," I explained. "I went and got these for you. I hope it is enough for everyone." Her angry expression softened, a tear forming in her eye. "I do need to explain that the manager decided he's not going to give you free food, anymore, even when we mess up an order. From now on, if you order from us, it will be at your own risk." I tried to keep an understanding voice, not wanting to offend her further. Still, I felt it was important she understood the situation. "There is a note in the computer to let everyone know, but I didn't want your kids to be hungry. I have one other thing for you."

"What?" She blinked tears away, wrinkles of confusion coming to her forehead.

I lifted a plastic bag which I had hidden against the wall near her door, handing it to her. The 2-liter bottle of neon green Mountain Dew was visible through the thin, white plastic. "I hope you have a good night."

She thanked me again, and I left the house. For the next two years, the family continued to order from us, never once calling to complain about the food, again.

TWO YEARS OF UNO

On the tail end of a snowstorm, late at night, one of our usual customers placed an order. It was larger than his usual, four pizzas instead of one or two. Late-night orders are not fun, orders where you have to worry about the snow...even less so. But I wasn't too worried. He was a good tipper—usually ten dollars minimum—and he didn't live far away.

Fifteen minutes later, I arrived at his house. I had to park on the street on the side of the house instead of pulling into his driveway. Otherwise, I risked getting stuck in the snow. Aside from the customer's car, I noticed two other cars at the house. *He must be having a party*, I thought to myself as I rang the doorbell.

He was quick to answer the door, not wanting me to have to wait in the snow, and he invited me in out of the cold. I declined the request: keeping an appreciative smile on my face, removing his food from the bag, and handing it to him. He took it, setting it down on an end table near the door.

"You need a pen?" I asked, pulling the credit card receipt from my pocket and handing it to him.

"No," he shook his head, pulling a pen from his pocket. "I have one." He signed the receipt, handing it back to me. "Drive safe."

"Always do," I nodded, observing his usual ten-dollar tip. "Have a good one."

"That's what paratroopers say."

"What?" I lifted an eyebrow.

"Have a good one." He repeated. "People in the military say that. That's where the phrase comes from. It started with paratroopers."

"Cool," I grinned as he shut the door. "Good to know."

As I returned to my car, I made a mental note to look up what he'd told me to see if it was true. According to what I found, it is. Who knew? I mean...apparently, he did.

When I got back to my car, I noticed a blue Uno card taped to the window, a number 2. At first, I felt confused, wondering where the card came from. Then it hit me. Someone must have snuck out the side of the house and placed it on my window while I interacted with the customer. I smiled, removing the tape and tucking the card into my pocket.

Less than a week later, the same customer ordered again. And again, it was my turn to deliver the food.

Before I knocked on his door, I removed an Uno card from my pocket, but it wasn't the same card. This one was a yellow 2. I slipped it under his windshield wiper and proceeded to the house.

When he answered, I handed him his food and told him. "That paratrooper thing you said was interesting. I read more about it."

"I learned it playing Call of Duty." He explained.

"Cool."

We finished the exchange, I returned to my car and drove back to the store.

Before my next work shift, I came in early, parked my car behind the store, and made myself some pasta in the store. About thirty minutes later, I left the store to take my first delivery. Sitting inside my wiper blade was a yellow Uno card, this one a number 4. I smirked, sighed, shook my head, and continued with my shift.

This game of Uno has continued for two years, now. We've done everything. +4 wilds with a second card attached, reverse cards with notes about how that means they have to do two cards next time, so on and so forth. The only thing is. I'm not sure how to determine when one of us has won.

THE WILD LIFE OF WILDLIFE

My wife was born in the Chilean city of Valdivia and raised in the town of Lago Ranco. It is a part of the world with an unmatched beauty, full of dark blue rivers and reflective lakes. Emerald trees stand tall, shadowing houses and road-ways. Full bushes and thick grass blanket every inch of the town. They line everything from roads to doorsteps. Red, copihue flowers dot every inch of vegetation.

Cheyenne lacks that natural beauty. When we were newlyweds, she would wake up in the mornings, look through the living room window of our small apartment, stare at our front yard, and declare. "Pucha, que Cheyenne es feo." Trans-lated, it means, "crap, Cheyenne is ugly."

What saved the city for her was the wild-life. Aside from some sea lions, I never saw wild-life where she lived. Cheyenne—on the other hand—is home to a variety of creatures, big and small. It is what she loves most about the town.

While delivering, I've seen various cotton-tail rabbits, hares, horses, pronghorn, longhorns, red foxes, cows, squirrels, sparrows, robins, crows, bison, and goats. Deliveries to the coun-try make it difficult to determine which animals might be domestic. I see a lot of them out there. But in the city, some of them leave no room to doubt. They are undoubtedly, mischievously, unapologetically wild.

One specific animal is the embodiment of this. At night, I see these peak their heads up from sewer drains. Like Pennywise, they watch, wait, plot, their only goal to make my food their food. Though I've never lost a pizza to any of them, it isn't for their lack of trying.

What is this animal? We'll get to that. Don't worry.

My most memorable encounter with them involves an apartment complex. It is one where five or six buildings—four apartments in each building—share a parking lot. When I pulled into that lot, I searched for a free parking space. Due to the smaller lot size, there was only one open space; it was next to the dumpster. I pulled into that spot and turned off the car. Without my car lights, the area was dark. An overcast night sky didn't even offer me moonlight by which to see. With care, I grabbed the delivery bag. But before I'd opened the door of my car, out of the corner of my eye, I noticed the dumpster's lid move.

That's what I'd thought, anyway. When I focused on the lid, it remained still. *Must have been my imagination*, I thought, *I need to stop listening to these scary stories on the radio*. I exited my car, delivery bag in my left hand, closing the car door with my right.

As I rotated to face the apartment building on the far side of the lot, the lid creaked behind me. It was a prolonged sound, reminiscent of an old rocking chair tipping slowly back. Creeeeek. I spun and looked... Four sets of eyes stared back. They glowed from the slit between the black, plastic lid and the green metal of the dumpster. I jumped back, a spurt of adrenaline supercharging my heart and muscles.

The lid pushed up a little more, and the faces became clear: black masks around the eyes, triangular ears, a wet, black nose, a white and gray face. Raccoons? Keeping my eyes on the creatures, I backed away from the dumpster. The lid lifted further, and one of them slid out, his fluffy, ringed tail waving as he touched the ground and took two steps toward me.

From there, it didn't close the distance between us. Instead, it kept pace. I took one step back. It moved the same distance toward me. We continued this dance until I reached a wooden staircase. As I ascended the steps, the trash panda remained at the bottom. From there, he watched, rubbing his hands together with palpable malice.

After I make this delivery, I wondered, *how should I approach the raccoon? Does it have rabies? Will trash pandas attack people? Is it like the squirrels in the park, and it is waiting for me to give it food? I do have some combos in the car...*

I rang the doorbell, and a man answered

the door. At some point during the transaction, he noticed the raccoon. Wrinkles of concern creased his forehead. "Guh, I hate those things. They don't let you take the garbage out without jumping out at you."

His words worried me, so I asked, "but they don't like actually attack you, do they?"

He laughed at the question. His laughter proved more concerning than his initial statement. While still smiling, he took the food, and closed the door.

The trash panda continued to watch, still rubbing its hands together.

With caution, and holding my bag in front of me as a shield, I crept down the steps...and it didn't move. Five steps between us... four... three... two...

It jumped away from me, spinning in the air, landing in a sprint, and fleeing back to the dumpster. In the shadows, I couldn't tell if it had joined its family inside the green box of metal, or if it had hidden somewhere else. For all I knew, it was waiting on the roof of my car, prepared to pounce.

I padded across the parking lot: heart beating heavy in my chest, wide eyes scanning the area around my car, my ears open to every sound. Wind pushed a bag of potato chips across the asphalt, rustling behind me, and I jumped again. *They're only raccoons*, I thought.

What harm can they do?

When my car door and the dumpster came into sight, I didn't see the trash pandas anymore. So I sped up, removing my car key from my pocket and unlocking the door. As the doors clicked, the headlights turned on, and the four raccoons became visible. Between a bush and the dumpster, they crouched, watching me.

Instead of going straight to my door, I decided I needed something to distract them. As such, I popped the trunk, whispering to myself, "good thing I did some grocery shopping today."

I pulled the bag of combos from the trunk, opening the bag before shutting the trunk. Then I drew a handful of the cheese-filled pretzel snacks and tossed them in the direction of the raccoons. Without hesitation, they snatched up three to four combos a piece, and standing on two feet, ran into the bushes. Until that point, I didn't realize trash pandas could run on two feet. It seems they can.

As I opened my driver's side door, I climbed inside, pulling the door shut. Once I'd reached the safety therein, I sighed to myself. Then I wondered what those raccoons would have done to me if I didn't have a snack to offer them.

BIG BILLS

One of the first customers I met, became a regular customer. He worked out of town, but when he returned to Cheyenne, he ordered every night. For the purpose of this story, I'll refer to him as Charleston.

The first time I delivered to Charleston, he answered the door with a book in his hand, <u>Words of Radiance</u> by Brandon Sanderson. As a Sanderson fan myself, we began to talk about the book. Throughout that conversation, he mentioned he was writing his own fantasy novel. If I didn't have to get back to the store, we could have talked about literature and writing for hours.

When he paid for his order, he used a fifty-dollar bill to pay for twelve dollars of food. When I explained I only had twenty dollars in change, he told me to give him what I had and keep the rest. It totaled out as an eighteen-dollar tip.

Back at the store, the manager was quick to examine the fifty-dollar bill, explaining. "People like to pay with big bills and tell you to keep the change. That way, you get excited for a big tip, forgetting to check if the bill is real." In Charleston's case, the fifty was legitimate, and the big tip became his norm.

Yet, my manager taught me a valuable lesson; I needed to be more careful with accepting large bills. Over the next five years, I've come across a few forgeries. The story which follows is one of those instances.

I received a call, and the man on the line placed an order. "I want three medium pepperonis on hand-tossed crust, three two liters—one coke, one root beer, one sprite—a chicken bacon ranch sandwich, and an alfredo bowl in a dish... How much am I at?"

"Forty-dollars," I gave the total. I don't actually remember the exact items or total, but it was close to this.

"I'll need change for one-hundred dollars."

"I'm sorry, Sir," I apologized, "we only carry twenty dollars in change. Due to recent rule changes, a driver won't be able to bring more change than that."

"What about a fifty?" He asked, his tone showing he understood the policy.

"Since it is a forty-dollar order, we'll be able to make up the ten-dollar difference," I confirmed.

He gave me a hotel's address and room number. Before I hung up the phone, the manager had begun to prepare the man's food. Ten minutes later, I left the store with the order.

When I arrived at the hotel, a man waved me down in the parking lot, so I pulled up to him, rolling down my window, "how can I help you?"

"I ordered the food." He explained, holding up a fifty. "I ordered the pepperoni pizzas, sodas, sandwiches, and pasta."

"Right," I nodded, keeping my best customer service voice. "Let me park real quick."

"Sure," he stepped back, and I pulled into the nearest spot.

After I handed him the food, he gave me the fifty. As has become habit, I checked the fifty. In the space where a fifty has a declaration that it is official tender, this bill stated that it was prop money. Aside from the statement, it looked like a legal bill, so I gave the man the benefit of the doubt. Maybe he didn't realize it was fake. I held it up to him. "This says it is prop money."

He swore aloud, turning to run and keeping the food balanced in his hands. Instead of going to a hotel room, or a car in the parking lot, he went toward a truck. It was parked along the street. It's lights flashed on, and the back driver's side door opened. And the man jumped in as the truck began to drive away, I looked at its license plate. Once I got in my car, I wrote down the plate number, drove back to the store, and called the cops.

Thirty minutes later, an officer had the man in the back of his car, and I was identifying him.

I'm not sure there is a moral to this story, but I miss the tips Charleston used to give. I miss him. Does anyone know where he is? Is he okay?

Josh Walker

JONNY PILLOWHANDS

April is a busy time at my house. It is a time when I prepare for the end of the school year, a time when I get ready for my middle child's birthday.

Speaking of my middle child, I remember going to the open house at the beginning of his Kindergarten year. His teacher was the same one who taught my oldest daughter, a fantastic teacher. I was glad he'd be in her class. When we arrived at her classroom, we spoke to her for a few seconds. Then we went to find my son's seat.

There were four or five circular tables in the room. The tables had spots set at their edges, each place with a name marker for the child who would sit there. After a few minutes in the room, I noticed a new family walk in, an adult man and woman—both about my age—and a little girl. She searched for her spot and found it, the spot to my son's right. My son noticed her Frozen backpack and began to talk to her about it. Since it is one of his favorite movies, the girl and my son became fast friends.

I took a second glance at the couple who came in with the girl. I recognized the man, a parent from my days working at Head Start. "Jesse," I nodded to him, smiling. "How have you been?"

At first, he didn't recognize me, confusion inherent in his eyes, but his disoriented state didn't last long. Within seconds, clarity returned to his face, and he smiled, "Mr. Josh, it's good to see you. Is your kid in this class?"

After some pleasantries, he introduced me to the woman who came in with him, saying her name was Tiffany.

Over the next few weeks, I met Tiffany's ex. He was the girl's biological dad. I also met Tiffany's mother. At the end of each school day, Tiffany's mom, the classmate's father, Tiffany, or Jesse would wait in a line to pick up the girl. To pick up my son, I also had to wait in the line. It gave me a chance to get to know them.

We'd talk about how work was going, I learned about how they enjoyed going to Rockies games, so on and so forth.

Jump ahead to April. One night, I had a few things in my head. First, I thought about my son's birthday. *What presents did I still need to buy? What cake should I get? Where should we have a party?*

In the back of my mind, I worried about a snowstorm. It would hit in the early morning, and I was working a closing shift. I hoped to get out before the snow started, so I came into my shift and began working on dishes right away. I figured if I could do five to ten minutes of work between each delivery, I'd finish dishes fifty minutes sooner.

The night proved slower than usual, allowing me to finish the dishes before close. That is to say, it allowed me to finish everything other than the closing dishes. I'd still have to wait to wash the peel, one of the cutters, the bubble fork, and a few other things.

When I reached this point, I moved to help with the front of the store, looking at the clock as I passed it. 11:30 PM. So far, so good, I thought to myself, I'll be home before 1:00.

I started washing down the cut table, and time crawled. 11:35, still no orders. I finished cleaning the cut table and began to sweep the area around it. 11:40. All is well, I smiled, we will get out before the storm. 11:42...the phone rang.

When a call comes in, our computer displays the name and address of the last person who ordered from that number. So I tapped the touchscreen to view the information. It came up, and I answered the phone. "Thank you for calling Pizza Place. This is Josh. How can I help you?" I said this as I look at the address. It was a street about five minutes away from the store. Next, my eyes snuck a glance at the name of the previous person who ordered. Tiffany. It's a common enough name, no last name attached. I confirmed the name and address and verified the call back number.

At that point, I didn't realize it was the

same Tiffany from my son's class. I had no reason to. The school boundaries for my child's
school were outside my delivery area.

After Tiffany placed the order, I added a
coupon to save her three dollars. She didn't ask
for the coupon, but when I can, I try to help the
customers save some money.

Once I hung up, I made the pizza and
tossed it in the oven. By 11:55, I'd pulled the pizza from the oven, cut it, slid it in a pizza bag, and
made my way to the car.

At exactly midnight, I got to the house, still
hoping I could get home before the snow started.
I didn't see anywhere to park in front of the two
buildings, so I forwent the parking lot, stopping
on the curb along the street. It was about a quar-
ter of a block up.

As I opened my car door, I noticed the
temperature outside had dropped twenty degrees from when I left the store. To this day, I
don't think I've ever seen the temperature drop
so fast. It made me shiver and regret my choice
to wear short sleeves.

I scanned the apartment complex for the
address they'd given, identifying it as the bottom
right unit. The same unit had on the porch light. I
could see the lights on inside the house, too, and
shadows moving behind the curtains.

I moved up to the place; the door had a
sign taped to it. The sign talked about avoiding

loud noises because someone in the home had autism. As someone who is on the spectrum, I appreciated the warning and knocked quiet. Then I waited.

In most circumstances, I don't have to wait long. People are waiting by the door for their food and answer within the first few seconds. Sometimes a child will shout from the inside, "mom, the pizza is here." Less patient children open the door themselves only to have their parents reprimand them for not waiting.

None of that happened. Five seconds went by. Then ten. Due to the sign on the door, I didn't want to ring the doorbell. I considered texting the number to let them know I'd arrived. Fifteen seconds. Did I need to knock, again? Twenty seconds.

As I lifted my arm to knock a second time, the door opened. It left me with my bag in one hand and my other hand about to bang on the customer's forehead. She laughed at the strange position. As quick as I could, I played it off, lowering my hand, shifting the bag, and removing her pizza.

It was then the smell of marijuana hit me. It was a familiar smell for a late-night delivery, so I shrugged it off, no big deal. Then I recognized who had answered the door. It was Tiffany, the same from my son's class. She smiled, said, "I'll go get them for you. They'll be right out," and she hurried to a back room. She didn't even take the pizza with her.

This is always weird for delivery drivers. In my head, I'm saying, 'wait, you mean to tell me you called, placed the order, and answered the door. Yet, the food isn't for you? Okay. Whatever. So long as I get paid for it.' What was even weirder was she seemed to be in such a hurry that she didn't even recognize me.

After another minute or two of waiting, she emerged from the back room. Jesse followed her, along with someone who I didn't know. While Tiffany and the other man waited back, Jesse came up to me. With glazed eyes and slurred speech, he took the pizza. "how much was it?"

"16.36," I answered him.

He began to dig in his pocket, all the while wobbling back and forth. I thought he might fall over, and he was a large man. If he did topple over, I'd try to catch him, but I wasn't sure I could hold him up. Like Tiffany, he didn't seem to recognize me. I guess people don't expect to see the parents of their children's classmates during random encounters at midnight. While Jesse continued to remove the money from his pocket, I asked him and Tiffany about their kids.

At that point, they paused, taking a closer look at me. It didn't take them long to recognize me, and we filled the next few seconds with awkward conversations. Tiffany didn't say it, but I could tell she was embarrassed. I guessed for the marijuana smell. Though I couldn't be sure. With hampered dexterity, Jesse pulled out a twenty, extending it to me. "keep the change."

The man who I didn't know—I later learned his name was John—decided that was a good time to push past Jesse. It caused Jesse to stumble to the side. If not for the doorframe, Jesse would have fallen over.

Tiffany told John to be careful and call when he got home.

John also had glazed eyes, a fact that didn't surprise me. What did draw my attention to him was his aviator's hat with earflaps. He had the flaps down, a turtleneck pulled up to his nose, so I could hardly see his face. John looked at the twenty in Jesse's hand as Jesse handed it to me, but only for a second. Then his eyes shifted quickly away. John continued through the parking lot and toward the street, walking with slouched strides. In a way, they resembled dancing.

The drunkness of it lacked any rhythm, but I recognized that kind of walk. It is a movement a person uses to hide how tall they are. He headed straight toward my car, and I realized I'd need to be careful around him.

Even so, I wasn't worried. I'd locked the car, and even if I didn't, I never kept anything valuable in it, less so while delivering. I don't even bring my wallet to work with me, only my license. That license, I keep in my back pocket.

Also, John saw how I knew Jesse and Tiffany. Who would be crazy enough to try something when they no longer have anonymity? I took the twenty dollars from Jesse, tucking it into my front left pocket. As Jessie shut the door, I turned toward my car.

John was halfway between my car and the apartment, on his way back to the house. "I forgot something," he stammered as he stumbled along. I suspected he had tried to open my car, but found it locked. Unsuccessful, I guessed he'd return to the apartment, and that would be that.

But he didn't go toward the apartment, he came toward me, still doing his weird, slouching, dance walk. Even with him hiding his height by doing this, I recognize he was no taller than 5'6. If I had to guess, I'd say 5'4. Though he'd covered his face, he hadn't his body, and I don't believe he weighed more than 120 lbs.

When he was about ten feet away, I tried to make conversation with him, "you can feel that cold front moving in, huh?"

He paused at the question but didn't answer, squinting his eyes, keeping his face in the turtleneck. I moved my eyes to his hands, assuring he didn't have anything in them. He didn't. Yet, his pants were baggier. They could hide a weapon. Even so, he didn't seem dangerous.

He reminded me of people I'd encountered daily when I was a missionary in Chile.
Drunks always stumbled up to us and asked for
money. At most, I expected the same from him.
He'd ask for money. I'd explain I didn't have
much on me. I only had the $3.00 I'd brought in
case Jesse needed change and the twenty Jesse used for the pizza. $23.00 in total.

After a few seconds, John resumed his
walk and spoke. "Hey, I that twenty dollars…saw…do you think you could…"

I waited, not sure if he had finished speaking, keeping my eyes on his hands. He kept
them out of his pockets. He understood I
wouldn't let him close if I couldn't see his hands.
They were still empty, and I didn't recognize him
as being crazy enough to try something.

He was small, too drunk—maybe too
high—to stand up. I gave him a few seconds to
finish what he had begun saying. He didn't finish
it. Instead, he kept moving toward me, about five
feet away before I decided I had to break the si-
lence. "Sorry, this is the store's money. I don't
have anything I can give you."

My legs never broke stride, and at this
point, I had moved passed him, keeping him in
my peripheral vision. In part, I didn't want to
spend more time with this guy than necessary.
Also, I still hoped I'd get back to the store in time

to finish sweeping, mopping, and putting the makeline back together. My goal remained; I wanted to get home before the storm hit.

Good thing I kept John in my peripheral vision because as I went past him, he lunged. His left hand swung at the back of my head. By reflex, I rolled with the blow, deflecting it off my shoulder. Even if I hadn't defended, I doubt it would have caused much damage. My seven-year-old daughter punches harder than John. Instead of pulling his left arm back, he grabbed my shoulder with it. I could have pulled away, but for some reason, I was still worried about being polite.

Instead, I turned my shoulder to him, placing my feet in a guarding stance. My eyes tracked as he tried to use his other arm to swing toward me.

His slow, comical movements seemed out of place. It was like they belonged in a three stooges skit. I'd been in competitive martial arts competitions and MMA bouts. In those, people strung together fluid combos, disguising movements. This guy's punches came via 3-5 day standard mail. And it was apparent he didn't pay for the insurance.

I knocked his left arm away, yelling, "KII-AAHHP!" Then I blocked his right fist as he flung it at me two times, "KII-AAHHP, KII-AAHP!" I'd hoped the yells might scare him away, or draw the attention of someone who could help. No luck.

When he threw his fourth punch, I dropped my pizza bag and did something called a brush block. In essence, it pulls the person forward by their wrist and elbow, knocking them off balance. This sent him flying past me. He landed with a dull crack, face-first on the concrete.

I reached into my pocket, pulling out my keys and hitting the panic button. My car's alarm began to blare. If the yelling didn't get people's attention, I thought the alarm would.

John's eyes widened, and he tried to make up some story, "I thought you called me *****. I always punch racists, but now I know you aren't racist." Yup, that's what he said.

With race issues being so prominent in recent years, it bothered me the flippancy with which he used race as a defense. When people do that, it detracts from actual issues of racism. The Boy Who Cried Wolf comes to mind.

"Tiffany and Jesse are going to know who you are," I told him. "I'm calling the cops." I reached in my other pocket and pulled out my cellphone, keeping my eyes on his hands, making sure he still didn't have a weapon.

"I don't know them in that apartment," he pointed at the apartment from where he came, "I don't know Jesse and Tiffany there. Never been there before."

109

I rolled my eyes and backed up in the direction of my car, keeping my eyes on him. At this point, a truck passed by on the street. I'm not sure if the random passerby, the threat of the police, or the sound of my alarm scared off John. But at that point, he struggled to get up and stumble-ran in the opposite direction.

I called the police, and they ticketed John for intent to harm. If he punched with more strength than an angry three-year-old, he would have received a higher charge. In this case, his wimpiness was his salvation.

At the kid's school the next day, I spoke to Tiffany. That's when she told me John's name. Upon learning it, I laughed, insisting she refers to him as Jonny Pillowhands. She agreed.

When I had a follow-up call with Officer King, I asked him to also use the name Jonny Pillowhands. He laughed and agreed. From what I understand, John's social circles continue to refer to him as Jonny Pillowhands.

All said and done, the worst thing that happened that night wasn't the interaction with Jonny Pillowhands. The worst part came in having to take time out of my night to deal with him. I had to call the police, recount my story multiple times. After it was all said and done, that 12:30 A.M. close became a 2 A.M. close. At the end of the night, I didn't get home before it started to snow. Thanks a lot, Jonny Pillowhands.

WE JUST WANT TO MAKE YOU HAPPY

We have the best customers. It's the truth. I have no doubt about it. Sure, every now and then, we get a scammer. Yet, statistics and my own subjective experience, indicate scammers are outliers. 90-95% percent of the complaints we get are legitimate and fair. In those circumstances, we want to be honest and take care of our customers.

As such, this is another story I hesitate to share. But some scammers need to be called out; their stories prove too shameless to ignore.

One night, a call rang in, and I answered it. "Thank you for calling Pizza Place. This is Josh. How can I help you?"

"Your other store won't fix their mistake. The manager yelled at me and said she wouldn't fix it, but she messed it up. I wanted to know if your store can fix the mistake?"

Our store has a note in the computer, I will paraphrase it as much as possible. Keep in mind, in these notes, my store is the east store:

"South store replaced woman's food on four separate occasions. On the fourth time, we took pictures of food before sending it out. We checked everything she has complained about in the past. We reviewed these things twice. We did this for every item sent out. Even so, the woman called back. She wanted replacement food sent out, claiming we undercooked the food.

"This time, we said we'd need the food back, but we could replace it.

"Customer said she already ate it, and couldn't return it. But she said we undercooked it and she needed more.

"We replaced it, explaining to her how we'd taken pictures and quality checked her order. We explained we keep a recorded history of all orders, including free ones. We told her that she hadn't been a paying customer for well over a year. As such, we explained we would no longer replace orders with her.

"Days later, she ordered again, complained, and we didn't give her replacement food.

She proceeded to call the north store, complaining to them. The north store called me to see what had happened. When I explained it, the north store had already sent out a driver to replace her food for free. Driver told her that his store would not do it again.

"Four days later, the woman ordered from us again. She called back, asking for free food. We refused it. She called the north store, and they called me back, letting me know she'd tried to do it again, and they denied it.

"The east store called me, seeing what

had happened, explaining they had replaced her food. I told them the situation, and they said they would not replace it again.

"I sent this out to all managers in my area, asking them not to replace this woman's food."

After reading the note in the system, I checked the order history, confirming it. Then I told the woman, "I'm sorry, mam, I won't be able to help you replace food from the other store."

"Please," she asked, "it was so bad, my daughter had to go to the emergency room. She's sick there, now."

"I'm sorry to hear that. If that is the case," I explained, "We need to get the pizza back from you. I'll have to check with the manager to verify this. Yet, I am almost sure we have to lab test any of our food that makes someone sick, so we can prevent it from happening again."

"We already ate it, and now she is sick." The woman said.

"I'm sorry," I decided to put the reflective listening skills I learned as a missionary to good use. "If I understand, you ordered it, and every-one ate it until it was gone. Though your kids are still hungry because they didn't eat it? Getting a new one is the only way to feed them? And somehow, even though they didn't eat, your daughter did eat it, and it made her sick?"

"Mom," I heard a voice in the background, "Did you tell them I'm in the hospital? You need to be honest, mom. This is embarrassing. Did you say you have other kids, too? I didn't know I have siblings. Do you do this while I'm at college, too? Lie to people for food?"

The mom ignored her daughter and told me. "We are in the hospital, and my other kids didn't eat it because I threw it away when my daughter got sick."

There are moments in time where it is hard not to feel insulted. There I was, on the phone with a woman who kept changing her story, lying and trying to scam every slice of pizza she could from us. To top it off, she thought she could change her story, and no one would notice.

And there I was, someone who speaks two languages and understands three, someone who has written five novels, three of which were Amazon best sellers. On top of that, I'd done one novella and was an editor on two anthologies. I had short stories published in two other collections. I'd done interviews on Chilean National Television. A magazine in Bangladesh had published one of my essays. I'd worked on video game stories, and did social work for eight years. And this woman saw me as an absolute moron.

"Since you threw it away, and didn't eat it," I said, "I will need you to dig the pizza out of the trash, so we can have it tested. Also, I heard what your daughter told you."

"**** you!" She hung up. I noted the experience in the computer and sighed.

Two seconds later, the phone rang, again, "hi, this is Charleston. Is that you, Josh?"

"Charleston!" I smiled, "brother, I thought aliens kidnapped you or something. Where have you been?"

"After I punched Jake," I didn't know who Jake was, "I moved to Ft. Collins. It's too embarrassing to be around Jake anymore. I'm in Cheyenne, visiting a friend for the weekend. Listen, I picked up a pizza today, and they messed up the toppings. Could I come in and exchange it for the proper pizza."

"Keep the pizza you have." in three years of ordering almost nightly, he had never asked for a replacement, so I knew it was us who messed up. Plus, that is the case more than 90% of the time. Until people force us not to, we'll always give them the benefit of the doubt. "I'll make you whatever you want as a replacement, on us."

"What do you mean anything I want?"

"Pick the toppings and crust. If you want what you ordered before, I'll make that. If you wanted a bigger pizza with more toppings, I'll do that. Whatever you want, man."

"Ah," he laughed, "Cool. In that case…"

THE GREAT RACE

When considering rare, positive experiences, one remains highlighted in my memory. It happened on a busy night in late April. I returned to the store to see Deku, the manager. Under normal circumstances, he didn't wait for drivers to return from deliveries, not in the parking lot, anyway. Yet, there he was, standing by the back door. His eyes were wide, a mix of panic and excitement in them. As I parked, he held his arm bent in front of him with his pointer finger out. From that position, he rolled his forearm in quick, tight circles, gesturing for me to hurry. Then he retreated into the store.

I parked my Malibu, removed the key, jumped out of the car, and slammed the door behind me. While I ran to the store, I clicked my keyfob, locking my doors, not sure what waited for me.

When I entered the store, Deku met me three steps in. He stuck a tag to my shoulder, telling me to trade my empty pizza bag for the one he held. When we switched bags, he explained, "it is a race. They ordered from five pizza places at once. We have to win. All your sides are in the bag; it's a cash order; go!"

"Yessir," I turned, speeding back to the car. My heart beat faster. Adrenaline rushed through my blood. My senses sharpened. I didn't want to lose. Yet, after I climbed in the car and placed the pizza bag in the passenger seat, I looked at the order. At which point, I realized I was at a disadvantage. The customer placed the order fifteen minutes earlier. This meant the food had been ready to go for eight minutes with no driver in the store to take it. No doubt, the other pizza places would be doing their best to win, too. Why couldn't the customer have ordered eight minutes later? I would have had those eight extra minutes.

Without wasting time, I buckled up, started the engine, put the car in drive, and began toward my new destination. While driving, I like to set cruise control, so I don't speed by accident. During that delivery, the speed limit seemed excruciatingly slow. To not speed, it took a superhuman act of willpower. A car topper helped me remember I represented the brand. Thoughts of my kids reminded me I had greater responsibilities than winning a pizza race…

…Yet, I didn't want to lose.

The route took me north across the county line, dirt roads running east and west along the way. On a typical delivery, I would have had the delivery in my GPS, but I didn't have time for that. Instead, I had to watch those side streets. In the dark, it didn't leave much time to react. To help with this, I watched for Columbia Rd. It was the road that came before the one where I needed to turn. At Columbia, I slowed down, looked for the next street sign, and flipped on my blinker. Then I turned east. Under the influence of precipitation, the dirt road had turned to mud. My car's worn, front struts rattled as I moved through divots and puddles. To counteract the rain, my wiper blades swiped back and forth. Woosh. Woosh. Woosh.

The address was an even number, so I knew it would be on the north side of the road. I'd also guessed that someone who ordered so many pizzas would have lots of cars in front of the house. A few homes in, I found one which matched the conditions: well lit, lots of cars out front, on the north side of the road.

The address on my tag matched the one on the mailbox. That was the house. With a hard crank of the steering wheel, the car pointed down the driveway. My headlights illuminated the cars therein, and my heart sank.

Another delivery car sat in the parking lot, its car topper taunting me. The topper wasn't lit up, so I hadn't noticed it before. By how much did they beat me? Would the eight minutes have made a difference? Was I second place? Was I fifth?

I found a spot to park where I wouldn't box in the other driver or cars. At the same time, I would be able to get out after I made the delivery.

With a humbled dejection, I got out of my car, closed the door, and took two steps toward the house. At that point, I heard a woman shout. "You got second place; he only beat you by thirty seconds." My eyes scanned toward the voice. In the dark, I hadn't noticed her before. A woman with shoulder-length blonde hair stood near a door that opened into the garage.

"Thirty seconds..." I mumbled to myself and sighed, hastening my pace to reach her. "Second place..."

She asked, "Can you come in?"

Under normal circumstances, we don't go into houses. It's a rule for our own safety. Even so, at this point, I noticed a sign in the window. If memory serves me, it read Young Life Ministries. This home doubled as a church, or at least, a place where church activities took place. We can deliver inside businesses and churches. I've done so countless times before, so I considered this to be the same. "I can go in," I answered her, "where would you like me to place the food?"

"It'll be a few minutes," she told me. "Then I'll show you." She guided me into a well-lit garage, one that was wide enough for four vehicles but only housed two. Aside from some tools hanging on the walls, it was empty. To the right was a closed-door that connected to the house. On the other side of the door, I could hear cheering and laughing. "When they finish," she explained, "it will be your turn. Don't ask the other driver to tell you what happened. It needs to be a surprise."

"Right," I agreed. After a minute or so, the door opened, and the driver from the other pizza place came out.

"You're in for a treat," he chuckled as he turned toward the door that took him outside.

"You're up," the woman gestured toward the open door. "Have fun."

As I stepped in, she closed the door behind me, leaving me in a room full of people. Most of them were teenagers who wore Young Life t-shirts. Some were adults. They all clapped, cheered, and shouted. One of the adults stood near the door where I entered. They pointed to a table on the opposite side of the room, "you can put it over there."

I nodded and took a few seconds to plan how to reach the table. The kids filled most of the room, blocking any straight path. Or so I thought. No sooner had I begun toward the table when the kids stepped to each side, forming the pathway which wasn't there before...I strode down it. The cheering continued, and kids on each side of me pulled out streamers. They were the kind where you pull a loop, triggering a pop that shoots out the strips of paper. Confetti filled the air around me, some landing on my head and shoulders.

Halfway to the table, I saw a woman standing near where I would set down the pizzas. When she began lifting her hand to her face, I noticed a microphone. "And in second place, we have Pizza Place! Everyone, give a round of applause for their driver as he makes his way to the winner's circle."

When I reached the table, I removed four pizza boxes from the bag. Up to that point, I realized I hadn't even checked the order. Deku promised me he had, and under the circumstances, I trusted him. Even so, as I placed the boxes down, I verified the tags, assuring the whole order was there.

The second I'd set the pizzas down, the woman with the microphone stepped next to me. She held the mic between us, asking, "how did you get second place today? What is your secret?"

Before answering, I turned toward the crowd of kids. Their cheering had stopped. Infinite sets of eyes stared straight at me, anxious, awaiting an answer. How should I answer a question like that? "Uh...eh...I drove here..." Great job, Josh. That wasn't a lame answer, I chided myself.

"He drove here!" The woman repeated, and cheers erupted. Three of the kids stepped forward. One paid me for the order, including a twenty-dollar tip. The second handed me a tro-phy. In a past life, it had been a basketball tro-phy. In sharpie, they'd written over the original engraving – 2nd place Young Life Pizza Race. The third of the children handed me a poster made of red construction paper. Messages filled the poster, each message signed by one of the kids. Their words expressed appreciation for the work I did. At the top of the poster read, Pizza Place. A hand-drawn store logo was next to the store name.

When I exited the house and garage, I re-alized no other drivers had arrived. Though, the driver who won first place waited for me near my car. "I have a confession," he told me as I ap-proached.

I smiled, knowing he had been through the same experience as me. It was something hard to appreciate in full, but I knew he could. It had put me in a great mood. I was sure he felt the same. "A confession?" I repeated, prying, "what's the confession?"

"This is an annual thing they do." He laughed. "I got second place last year, so this year, I've been following their Facebook page. I saw the flier they put up, so I knew they were do-ing this tonight. I wasn't scheduled, but my man-ager let me come to the store and wait for the order. I waited for three hours to take this single delivery. The second it came in, we sped to make it. We already had large dough out and ready for the pizzas. As soon as the order came out of the oven, I was on my way here. Even so, you still almost beat me. I wanted to let you know that under any other circumstances, you would have won. As far as I'm concerned, you got first place. You should change that on your trophy."

I thanked him for his words, and we both went back to our cars.

When I returned to the store, Deku waited for me, "did we win?" He asked, eyes wide and hopeful.

"Second place," I told him.

He frowned and hung his head.

I tried to raise his spirits, explaining how the store that got first place knew about the race ahead of time. I told him how the driver who beat me admitted we should have won. Then I proceeded to use a dry erase marker to write over the, '2nd place,' on the trophy. This made the sharpie erasable, and off I wiped it. Then I wrote 1st place where 2nd place had been. If the guy who won thought I deserved first place, who was I to argue?

I've since begun to keep an eye on Young Life's Facebook page. Due to COVID-19, they canceled the race this year. Though, you can be sure that when they do it, again, I will come away with an undisputed first place trophy.

DELIVERY FAILED

Drivers have a certain amount of discretion when it comes to completing deliveries. About once a week, we come to a house, we knock on the door, and the customer doesn't answer. In those cases, we look at the phone number and give them a call. At this point, ninety-nine percent of the people answer the phone. Some of the more common reasons that they haven't answered the door are the following:

1. They are in the basement and didn't hear the door. It always seems to be the basement. I never hear people say, "I was in the attic and didn't hear the door." What is wrong with hanging out in attics? Would it be creepy if I said I hang out in my attic? I'm kidding, of course…except not. But I am. But not really.

2. They are on the way home and didn't realize I'd beat them to their house.

3. They forgot to update their address in the system. I need to go to a different house.

4. They are out back. I can go back and deliver it to them there.

5. By accident, they put down the wrong number for the house. They live two houses down.

6. They see me. They actually want me to bring the food to the corner of the block.

7. They are in the field across the street, hiding behind the tree stump. This one only happened one time.

Problems come when the person doesn't answer the door. Then we call them, and they don't answer the phone. At that point, we can wait a few minutes and try again. Though most drivers choose to return to the store with the food. If the customer wants the food, they'll call back and give us better information about how to find them.

When they don't call back, we zero out the order in the system. This includes nullifying credit card payments. Then we get to eat the food. Granted, with all the pizza I've eaten, it doesn't hold the same magic for me that it used to. It'll do in a pinch, but at this point, I'd prefer a salad...or cheese enchiladas. Then again, I prefer cheese enchiladas over anything.

Sometimes we take a delivery, and we don't have all the information. Even so, we have enough information to make the delivery. For example, the other day, I went to an apartment complex with four buildings. I had a room number, but not the letter to show in which building the customer lived. When I called for the building number, they didn't answer. It was mid-afternoon, so I decided to start in building A. From there, I would work to building D, knocking on the corresponding room number in each building.

Those buildings didn't have an elevator, and the room number was on the third floor. As such, I got a good work out before I found the customer in building C.

In reality, I've taken thousands of deliveries over the last five years. In all those, I've only failed to deliver the food a handful of times. Here are two of them.

The first of these came late one night. I arrived at the address and walked up to the apartment. Loud music blared from inside, a deep base thumping in a steady rhythm. Bum, dum, dum, bum, dum, dum, bum. A muffled voice accompanied the melody, but the base overwhelmed it all, so I couldn't make out the words.

I knocked on the door; no one answered. I rang the doorbell; no one answered. I shouted through the open window; no one answered. When a pause in the music came, I knocked again. Still no answer.

I'd left my phone charging in the store, and the apartment was only two minutes from the store, so I decided to go get my phone. Upon returning to the store, I called them, explaining I had been there.

The woman on the other side of the line explained she and her boyfriend were listening to music, so they didn't hear me. I told them I'd head back, but asked they be watching for me.

When I returned to their apartment, there was no music, and the apartment was dark. Two police officers stood in front of the door. One of the officers pointed at the apartment and asked me. "Is that food for them?"

"Yup," I answered monotone, nodding.

The officer laughed, turned, and knocked. I'm not sure I've ever heard anyone knock so loud before. "We know you are in there, and your pizza is here. Come get your pizza."

There was no response: no movement inside, no flickering lights, no sounds, nothing to indicate anyone was home. I called the number, and they didn't answer, but I could hear the phone ringing behind the door.

After my call went to voicemail, I left a message explaining we would cancel the order for them. Then I hung up and turned to the officers. "Do you two want these? It's on us. If you don't take them, we're going to throw them away."

With smiles, they declined. I returned a smile, shrugged, and went to my car.

Another time, it was an evening in October, not super late, but the sun had set. I had a note attached to my delivery. It read, deliver to the side of the house. When I arrived, I looked on both sides of the house. There were no visible doors. Rather, I encountered a tall fence on each side. Upon closer inspection, I noticed the fence on the east side had a gate. In the dark, the handle of it was easy to miss.

Since I didn't want to barge into someone's back yard by accident, I tried to call the number on the order. No one answered. A light shone through the front door of the house. As such, I decided try the front door before going through the gate. An older woman answered, saying, "oh, they're on the side of the house."

"Is the side door on the other side of the..." She shut the door on my face before I could finish my question, "...gate."

I hung my shoulders, made sure the address on the house matched the address of my order, and began toward the gate. It was one of those gates with the metal handle that has a release latch that you push down with your thumb. With caution, I held the latch down, pushed open the gate, and slid through the opening.

Without the streetlights, I couldn't see much, so I pulled my phone from my pocket, using its flashlight to illuminate the side of the house. About fifteen feet in was a door. *That's got'a be it*, I thought, turned off the flashlight and returned the phone to my pocket.

I should note that I didn't step far beyond

the gate without making sure I had a way to get to the alley. As a driver, we always keep our guard up, and if someone—or a group of someone's—ambushed me at the gate, I wanted another exit.

I maneuvered around some clutter. It came in the form of garden tools, a spare tire, and a bag of cement. Once I went to the door, I lifted my hand and knocked.

No one answered, so I waited thirty seconds and knocked, again.

This time I received an answer, but not at the door. Around the back of the house, I heard a growl.

As I turned my head toward the sound, a head came into view from the other side of the house, sharp teeth bared. In the dark, I knew it was a large dog, but I couldn't make out enough details to identify the species. Not that the species mattered. I had invaded this animal's space, it was territorial, and it was mad.

Keeping the bag between the dog and me, I backed toward the gate. One step back...two steps back. With my eyes up, I used my heel to feel for the tools, tire, and cement bag. When I bumped into one, I weaved around it. Five steps back...six steps back. I was almost to the gate.

The dog barked and charged, closing the distance between us in an instant, lunging at my shin. I dropped the bag, holding onto it by a side strap and letting it fall in front of my leg. It became a shield between the dog's bite and my leg. The animal's teeth tore into the pizza bag, the pizza box, and the pizza, poking holes into my pants...I worried about my leg. Yet, I knew I needed to get to safety before I could check for potential injuries.

While the dog thrashed, I was able to pull my leg away. The dog let go of the bag and stepped back. As it prepared to bite, again, I leaped back, grabbing the gate by the handle and slamming it shut. I felt the dog slam against the fence on the other side. The wood creaked and bent beneath his weight. I pulled on the handle one more time, making sure it latched before retreating to my car.

Once there, I examined my leg. It had bruised on each side of the shin, but the bite hadn't broken skin. I would be fine. However, that's more than I can say for the bag. The dog had torn it to shreds. Bits of melted cheese and red sauce stained the nylon fabric and cotton filling.

At that point, I drove back to the store, calling the manager and explaining the situation. Part of me wanted the person who ordered to call back, so I could figure out what happened. Did they give me the wrong address? Did a person who lived in the upstairs part of the house let a dog out, and a person who lived downstairs didn't realize the dog would be there?

Why didn't they pick up their phone when I called? After an hour, they still hadn't called the store about their delivery order. Why didn't they call back? Did they realize they'd almost fed me to their dog, and they felt embarrassed? Did they decide they didn't want to pay for a pizza that night? I never did find out.

COMMON CONVERSATIONS

CONVERSATION 1:

Me: Welcome to pizza place. Are you picking up or placing an order?

Customer: I'm picking up.

Me: What is the name on the order?

Customer: Roger.

Me: I don't see an order for Roger in the system. Could it be under another name?

Customer: No, Roger is the only name it would be under.

Me: Okay, what was in the order?

Customer: Three large pies. Two Pepperoni. One Cheese.

Me: Okay, I see an order like that, but it is under the name Pam.

Customer: That's it. Pam is my wife.

CONVERSATION 2:

Where this is a common scenario, customers tend to make the mistake based on estimated wait times. Most of the time, we tell them it will be 30-40 minutes for delivery. This is our lowest estimate we give. Even so, sometimes we arrive 15 minutes ahead of that estimate. In this situation, customers tend to tip well.

Me: *Rings doorbell and waits*

Me: *knocks on customer's door and waits more*

Me: *Calls customer's phone*

Customer: Hello?

Me: Hi, this is Josh from Pizza Place. I'm here with your food.

Customer: Oh! I thought it would take you longer. I'm about two minutes away. I'll be home soon. Do you mind waiting?

Me: That's fine. I can wait. I'll see you when you get here.

Customer: See you then *hangs up*

Me: *Puts phone in pocket and returns to car to wait*

Customer: *Pulls up to house fifteen minutes later*

CONVERSATION 3:

Customer: So they already tipped, right?

Me: No, Sir/Ma'am

Customer: But you get the delivery charge? That's what I mean.

Me: No, Sir/Ma'am

Customer: Well for what is the delivery charge?

Me: That helps to mitigate some of the store's costs associated with providing delivery as a service. For example, it pays for new hot bags, car toppers, insurance for the drivers, and things like that.

Customer: Oh... *signs credit card slip*

CONVERSATION 4:

Me: Thank you for calling Pizza Place. This is Josh. How can I help you?

Customer: I missed a call from there.

Me: *clicks computer to a list of delivery orders* Did you recently order food from us?

Customer: Yes.

Me: Can I ask the address?

Customer: 123 Make Believe St

Me: The call you received was from our automated system to let you know your food is on the way.

Customer: Cool, Thank you.

Me: Thank you.

CONVERSATION 5:

This is a specific conversation that happened, but variants of this are common. 99% of customers are understanding in this scenario. This specific customer was not.

Customer: *Places order an hour before we close the store*

Me: *attempts to deliver the order*

Customer: *Doesn't answer door*

Me: *Attempts to Call Customer*

Customer: *Doesn't answer phone*

Me: *texts customer*

Customer: *doesn't answer*

Me: *Calls Manager in store*

Manager: *Attempts to call customer*

Customer: *Doesn't answer phone*

Manager: *Calls me back*

Me: They didn't answer, did they?

Manager: Nope, bring it back to the store.

Me: *brings it back to the store*

Customer: *Calls store an hour after close*

Me: Thank you for calling Pizza Place. This is Josh. How can I help you?

Customer: I placed an order two hours ago, and it still isn't here.

Me: Are you at 123 Not-a-real St?

Customer: I am.

Me: I tried to deliver: knocked, texted, and called. We didn't get an answer.

Customer: I was here the whole time. You must have used the wrong number.

Me: Check your texts and missed calls from 123-456-7890.

Customer: Oh, I see those.

Me: That was me. I was at 123 Not-a-real St. Look at the second text. It is a picture of your house to show we were there.

Customer: Oh, I guess I zoned out.

Me: No worries, we did zero out the order on your card, though.

Customer: Could you remake the order and charge the card, again?

Me: Unfortunately, our ovens are off at this point, so I am unable to make anything. Also, we've put all the food away.

Customer: You can't turn them back on and get the food back out?

Me: We closed an hour ago. At this point we can't make new orders.

Customer: Well you messed up my order and I need my food tonight.

Me: Sir, I waited at your house for fifteen minutes, calling you, knocking on the door, and texting. When you didn't answer, I had to return to the store and continue working. If it will help, I can offer you a credit for some food tomorrow?

Customer: *swears and hangs up*

CONVERSATION 6:

This is a made-up example, but it represents the sentiment of a common situation.

Delivery Instructions: When driver arrives, have them do a rain dance to turn the earth into mud. Use the mud to build a pedestal. Wait for sun to dry the pedestal. Place food on pedestal. When food is in place, return to car and call.

Me: *begins to carry out instructions*

Customer: *opens door* What are you doing?

Me: *Still in the middle of rain dance* I'm...uh... doing what the deliver instructions said.

Customer: What instructions? You can hand it to me.

Me: *Makes confused face* Okay... *hands customer food*

COVID-19 EXPERIENCE

COVID-19 did a lot to our country, to the world. The funny thing is how quick people are to forget how they make up the world. Their actions and aspirations define it. Every choice a person makes has a consequence, some long-lasting... most insignificant. I don't refer to physical choices and consequences like wearing a mask and social distancing. Though, I do speak of social importance, or rather, the importance of being positive on a social level.

As history progresses, historians forget the definition of labels. And the meanings of words shift to a degree where no one remembers what they meant in the first place. What was a Republican one hundred fifty years ago? What was a Democrat fifty years ago?

Today, philosophers argue about such things. They twist history to match their preconceptions and derisive, tribal ideologies. I suspect COVID-19 will follow the trend. After all, we lived during it, and the only thing we agreed on is how the virus is harmful, even deadly.

For safety, we concealed ourselves in our homes. We isolated ourselves on social media. Some argued with those whom they called friends, cut their ties therewith. We hid from interaction; even though it is interaction that defines us.

Our ancestors hid, too. They inhabited caves, trapped in the dark for their own safety, isolated from potential danger. Where they were free from predators and harm, they were also devoid of friends. When cavemen emerged from the dark, they met their neighbors.

In some cases, their neighbors had learned to think differently. When conflicting ideas emerged, neighbors became competitors. They fought for resources, refusing to hear other opinions. They rejected the humanity in anyone who was not like them.

The world was hostile, angry, and confused. In reality, the world is a confusing place; that is its inherent nature. Another part of its nature is adversity. How we act in that adversity is how we show who we are.

We hadn't yet come to terms with COVID-19, and a new crisis came to the forefront of our society. A man was killed, and modern technology allowed the world to witness his murder. It was a horrible thing. On a personal level, heartache prevented me from watching the video in full. The barbaric nature of it disturbs everyone with whom I've talked.

Yet, like our species has always done, we nitpick. We focus on differences over similarities. We let anger continue to divide, negating the humanity we witness in those around us.

For a book about pizza delivery stories,

this is some deep stuff. I hope to find a purpose in it all. As an author, I seek out the stories around me, trying to see them in the smallest contacts and strangest actions. I try to find meaning in those experiences. As such, most of the chapters in this book focus on a single story or experience. Sometimes I expound on the lessons I learned from the experience.

This chapter is different in that it will focus on many of the smaller interactions I've had during the crisis. To be specific, I will be going over the events that occurred during one day of the crisis, and all the small things that happened that shift.

One of my favorite parts of delivering is talking to the customers. During the crisis, all deliveries were contactless by default. It prevented me from talking to anyone. On request, a customer could change to regular delivery, but few did. For carryout orders, we no longer allowed customers into the store. We had to wear masks, gloves, and learn the new systems. As drivers, it slowed us down a significant amount.

Even so, the mask I have is incredible. My wife is a cosplayer. While making costumes, she has gained some astonishing sewing skills. Using these, she made me the best Covid-19 mask in the store. It has scary, sharp teeth like a shark. Depending on if I wear it right side up or upside down, the teeth form a smile or a frown. I prefer the smile.

One night, during the last delivery, a kid saw my mask through the glass door to his house and shrieked with joy. His siblings ran to view it. They all seemed to love sharks. One of them even slipped by his mom, ran over to me, and hugged my leg. Kids are cool that way. They don't talk to strangers…unless that stranger has a shark mask. Then the stranger is their best friend. One of the kids pulled out a digital camera—I didn't know they still made those—and asked if he could take a picture. I told him that he could.

Aside from taking masks off and putting them on, again, other things made our delivery times slower, too. For example, the city shut down bars and dine-in options at restaurants. At that point, the number of orders we took was two to three times more than usual.

So let's jump ahead to that night near the beginning of the crisis.

I pulled up to the home of a regular customer, and the customer was waiting. She stood behind her screen door: arms crossed, frowning, glaring like an angry bulldog. From the time she placed the order to the time she received her food was forty minutes. We usually had it to her in twenty.

Before I could get a word out, she snapped. "I was going to give you a tip," she held up a white envelope with the name of my restaurant written across it. Then she tucked it into a coat pocket, "but you don't deserve it anymore."

This is a familiar mindset to me, and it is hard to fault those who have it. People who have to wait...they like to blame the driver. They don't realize that sometimes a driver will take three delivery orders at a time. Drivers manage the orders by distance and the time the customers have had to wait.

Sometimes the driver leaves the store with a single order that is twenty minutes old. Sometimes the driver leaves the store with three orders that are each forty minutes old. I have started a shift with a triple. I've also begun shifts with single orders that had been in the store for thirty minutes. The driver takes what the manager assigns them. Unless the driver gets lost on the way to the house, they don't determine how long a person waits for their food.

The next delivery I took was to an address east of town, about twenty minutes away from the store. A girl met me as I pulled up, wearing a t-shirt from her high school. When I asked her about it, she explained. "I'm graduating this year," adding, "I hope we will be able to have a normal graduation ceremony."

"I hope you'll be able to as well," I agreed, handing her the credit card slip.

High school students don't usually tip. Though, I wouldn't attribute this to malice. If anything, it is an honest oversight by their parents. As a parent myself, I understand. In this case, the girl signed the slip without much thought, handing it back and taking her food. Her age, along with the speed at which she signed the receipt, kept me from hoping for much. Yet, when I got back to the car, she had tipped $15.00.

The next delivery I took was contactless. The person who placed it didn't do a pre-tip on their credit card. 99% of contactless, no pre-tip, credit card deliveries signify I won't receive a tip. Still, I'd hoped they'd tape an envelope on their mailbox or something. They didn't.

Next, I delivered to a man at one of the nearby hotels. It was a contactless cash delivery. In those cases, I put food on a cardboard stand, knock, and stand back. Then the customers pick up the food from the cardboard stand, leave money in the stand, and return to their home. Or in this man's case, he returned to his hotel room. When I went to collect the money, he had shorted me three dollars. I tried to call him, tried to knock, tried to text. He refused to answer. I sighed. Three dollars wasn't worth a call to the police, and adding someone from out of town to our do not deliver list wouldn't do anything. I mean, someday he could come back to Cheyenne, stay in a hotel here, and try to order from us. Though, I doubted the likelihood of it. I felt powerless in the situation, but I sucked it up, returning to the store for my next delivery.

When I arrived at the next house, a man met me in his front yard. He cussed me out for taking so long and paid for the food with exact change, down to the penny. As I returned to my car, I sighed.

On that day, I took deliveries non-stop, 5:00 PM to 1:15 AM. Then I did dishes and cleaned the store for another two hours before going home. All in all, I took thirty-one deliveries that night and earned $27.00 in tips. My usual $15.00-$20.00 an hour became $6.25. Where I was usually home by 1:30 AM, it was almost 3:30 AM before I walked through my front door. It was a bad night.

Even so, I understood some of the vitriol that people felt. They weren't angry at me; they were mad at the virus. As I had felt powerless with the man who stole $3.00, these people felt powerless before COVID-19.

It dictated how they lived their lives, and they couldn't do anything to escape the situation. Their weakened emotional state caused them to act out. They scapegoated, projected, used other psychological defense mechanisms. They did it, so they could feel better.

When a person feels powerless, desiring change, hoping for things to get better, they must focus on the positive. That night, I could have carried my frustration with me. I could have held on to the anger I felt with the people who had mistreated me, had stolen from me. Instead, I focused on that high school graduate. She had her own preoccupations, but even so, she accounted for over half my tip money that evening.

This is my challenge for everyone who reads this. Be the change you want to see in others. Focus on the good you have in your life. Use that as fuel to overcome the bad. Project that goodness on others. Instilling kindness in others brings with it an exponential effect. It is more infectious than the virus itself.

As COVID-19 ends and a unity of races becomes a reality—maybe ten years from now, or one thousand—make historians look back on our time. Have them pinpoint it as one unlike any other in history, a time when humanity came together. Don't project your frustrations. Don't talk down to your neighbors. Don't belittle those who serve you. Understand. Uplift. Be kind. Respect. Personify the world you want to create.

HOLIDAYS

Pizza Delivery is one of those services that seems to always be open. In reality, we only close two days of the year, Christmas and Thanksgiving. During the other holidays—depending on which they are and the traditions associated therewith—we become extra busy. Or, in some cases, we become deader than my high school love life. This chapter will describe how different holidays impact the driving experience.

During Memorial Day and other three-day weekend holidays, we tend to have slower weekends. Though, we do get more deliveries to the KOA and other campgrounds in and around town. On Monday night, when people return home from camping, we get slammed. Those nights, we take three times the deliveries when compared to a regular Monday.

During the 4th of July, we also take many delivery orders to campgrounds. On one 4th of July, I had a drunk lady throw a plastic lawn chair at the side of my car. She thought I was going through the campgrounds too fast. Sorry, lady, I was only doing two miles per hour. If you hadn't been celebrating with plentiful amounts of certain beverages, you would have seen me before I was right next to you. Please, don't throw lawn chairs at me because you have impaired senses.

Speaking of celebratory drinking, during Saint Patrick's Day, I take many deliveries to bars. I'm someone who doesn't drink and never spent any time in bars. When I go to one on a delivery, I feel like a fish out of water. Do I go to the bartender and ask who ordered the pizza? They would know, right? Sometimes they do. Sometimes they don't. Sometimes they ordered it.

When the bartender doesn't know who ordered it, I pad around the bar. My eyes scan back and forth, searching for anyone who might be waiting for a pizza. When people see me do this, many claim ownership of the pizza. At which point, I ask the name on the order and the type of pizza they ordered. One time, I had this conversation four separate times before finding the order's actual owner. He was making out with a girl in the corner of the bar.

That brings us to Valentine's day, a slower than usual holiday. Custom orders make up for the slowness. Some people ask for us to shape pizza dough like a heart, or for us to spell out words with pepperonis.

Some of the busiest hours I've worked have been the hour immediately before the New Year. I understand this. Who wouldn't want to start the new year with pizza? If you answered that you wouldn't, you have no soul. Go get help.

As a side note, these New Year deliveries tend to be larger orders and bigger tips.

Halloween might be the most challenging holiday to work. There are kids in all the neighborhoods, so we have to drive very slow and careful. To top it off, people don't want to cook; they are busy getting their kid's costumes ready. As a result, Halloween becomes one of the busiest—if not the busiest—day of the year. Unless a driver has their own kids, the General Manager requires them to work.

Josh Walker

KENTUCKY

Of all the regular customers our store has, there was one who ordered more than any of the others. For the sake of this story, I'll refer to her as Kentucky. Sometimes she ordered twice a day, so everyone in the store knew her.

The first time I delivered to her, Psychologist asked if I had been there before. When I answered no, he replied. "You're in for a treat. She's a neat lady." Where some people might attribute sarcasm to his statement, I knew him well enough to know he was sincere in his assessment.

"Cool," I replied, looking up the address on our digital map. The arrow indicated a large building on the corner of two relatively busy streets. "Is it an apartment complex?"

"Retirement home." He explained. "Try to get there before seven. If you get there after that, you'll have to wait for her to let you in."

"Right," I took the order, loaded it in my car, and made my way to the complex. It took a while to find parking. I guessed because it was a four-story complex with a small parking lot. Instead of trying to find something close, I opted for a space on the far end of the lot. As I pulled into the spot, I checked the clock. It read 6:45 PM. I still had time to make it inside before they closed the front doors.

Once inside, I found myself in an open dining room with branching hallways. A staircase ascended to the left, and an elevator sat to the right. An empty receptionist desk rested by the door. I suspected this was due to the late hour. At the time, employees cleared off dining room tables. Who knows...the receptionist might have been one of them?

Some of the center's residents remained at the dining room tables, engaged in conversation. Others made their way back to their rooms.

As one older gentleman went by me, he made eye contact and chuckled, "Kentucky sure does like her pizza."

As he passed by, I offered a polite smile. Once he broke eye contact, I looked down at the receipt, reviewing Kentucky's room number.

It was on the second floor. A line of people—some of them in wheelchairs—waited for the elevator. So I chose to take the steps, climbing them to a balcony on the second floor. The balcony came in the form of a game area with a poker table, board games, comfortable chairs, and bookshelves. A white railing ran the length of the stairs and the balcony, allowing a person to see the dining area below.

When I looked down, I noticed a few of the residents looking up at me. Sometimes, when you deliver a pizza, you get funny looks. To deal with those looks, I have learned to pretend I belong and go about my business.

A hallway ran both ways from the gaming area. Directional signs affixed to it. Arrows on the sign pointed which direction to travel to find which room numbers. I followed the sign to the left, down the hallway, past some paintings. Some were of nature, others of ancient European style towns. One depicted a young girl in a bonnet and sky-blue dress. Around a corner to the left, I found the room and knocked.

"Come in," a woman's voice called. The tone was high pitched, and there was a tired, worn quality to it.

Inside the apartment, I saw the woman sitting in a motor-powered chair, oxygen connected to her nostrils. She told me to set the food on her fold-out couch in the living room, and I obliged. Then I handed her the receipt and a pen.

As she took it, she said, "you're new. What's your name?"

"Josh," I smiled.

"Josh?" she repeated my name as if rolling it over in her head. Then her eyes looked at mine. "I'm Kentucky. Did they tell you about me?"

"Only that you are a regular customer," I told her, trying to be diplomatic in my answer.

"I am the most regular customer." She laughed, signing the card slip and handing it back. "I love your spinach and feta pizzas. No one makes them better."

"Glad to hear it." I tucked the slip away. "You have a good night."

"You too, dear." She began to motor her chair toward the bed. "I'm sure I'll see you again soon."

She was correct. No more than a day later, I delivered to Kentucky a second time. With each delivery, I learned something new about her, and our conversations grew longer. I learned about how she always had pet cats, from the time she was a little girl to when she moved into the retirement center. She regretted not being able to bring her cats with her. Even so, she had children to take care of them, so she was grateful for that.

I learned she spent most of her adult life working in a factory where they put together munitions. She told me that she was a supervisor for most of that time.

One time, I delivered minutes after her VCR stopped working. She panicked because of this, showing me her VHS tapes, enough to fill four bookshelves. She worried she'd never be able to watch them again.

I ordered her a new VCR online, but before it came in, she'd already got a replacement from her online boyfriend. I didn't realize she had an online boyfriend, so we spent one of my deliveries talking about him.

During one delivery, she had a book out, reading about physics. To be specific, she read about the use of perpetual acceleration for space travel. After we talked about it, she asked where I'd learned about the concept. I explained I was an author and researched it while writing one of my books, <u>Phoenix Dawn and the Rise of the Witch</u>.

The next time I delivered to her, she had a copy of each of my books and asked me to sign them. I obliged.

In the store one night, we were on pace to finish with cleaning by 12:30 AM. About ten minutes before we closed, Kentucky called and placed an order. It was unusual for her to make an order that late, but we knew she would tip, and she was always kind to us, so we didn't mind.

After 8:00 PM, her building locks its front doors, so she would have to open them for us. Since I knew her health prevented her from moving quickly, I called her as I left the store with her food. It gave her a chance to get to the elevator and meet me at the front door of the complex.

"Josh," She answered her phone with my name. "I need to cancel my order. The battery on my chair broke. It will take me half an hour to get downstairs without it."

"Is there anyone who can help you there?

Any other way for me to get in?" I tried to problem solve. "if you think you can make it down safely, I'm happy to wait for you at the door."

"I can make it safely." She assured. "If you don't mind waiting. I'll do that. I'll head down now."

"Alright, I'll be there. Stay safe. Take as much time as you need." I told her. Then I took my time driving to the complex. It was the middle of winter, roads were slick, so the slower I could go, the better.

Even while driving slow, I arrived at the complex's front door twenty minutes before she did. As I waited for her, I passed the time playing solitaire on my cellphone.

When she finally did arrive, she looked better than I had expected. Aside from some heavy breathing, she had color in her cheeks and a wide smile. Once she let me in, I asked if she wanted me to walk with her back up to her room. If she preferred for me to go to her room myself and leave the food, I told her I could do that. I even offered to get her wheelchair and help her back to her room that way.

"The chair doesn't move right without the motor. The wheels lock." She sighed. "You wouldn't be able to push it. If you are in a hurry, you can leave the food in the room. It's late, and I understand."

"I'll walk with you." I smiled, and we began

toward the elevator. It didn't seem right to let her make the trip back up by herself.

As she walked with me toward the elevator, I realized she wasn't doing as well as she appeared. Her steps came slow, her legs wobbling, sweat forming beads on her forehead. "Do you mind?" She asked, supporting herself on my shoulder without waiting for the answer.

"That's fine," I told her.

We inched our way to the elevator, up to the second floor, and over to the game area. "I need..." she spoke between shallow breaths, her voice trembling, "to sit down."

"Right," I set her food on the poker table and pulled out a chair for her.

She thanked me and sat, and I sat across from her at the poker table.

After that, I don't remember what we talked about. Yet, I remember the feeling which accompanied the conversation. Her eyes seemed to reminisce as she spoke, remembering past interactions on cool summer nights, recalling a childhood. There was a reverence to it all...and a loneliness.

When she told me, "I'm ready to go, now," the tone in her voice carried a sadness. I'm sure she would have been able to talk all night, but she respected that my manager waited for me in the store. And she understood how I needed to get back home to my family.

I stood and helped her to her feet.

By the time we reached her room, it was 1:45 AM. "I'll let you eat this before it gets too cold," I told her, nodding at the food as I set it on her end table. "It was good talking to you. Have a great night."

"You too," she told me as she shut the door.

That was the last time I delivered to Kentucky. A few weeks later, she fell, suffering an injury that has her in a lifecare center.

I hope she recovers soon, returns to her room on the second floor where she can continue to order from us. If she doesn't, I am grateful for that last conversation we shared that late winter night.

Someone asked if there is a deeper meaning behind this story. If anything, I'd say it is to respect people. Everyone came from somewhere. They have a past. They have history. Their story is unique and important.

This applies to kids, to the elderly, to the disabled, to those who are like us, and to those who are different. People are amazing, and each one has something to teach us.

AFTERWORD

The other people with whom I work have their own stories, countless stories, too many to include in this book. Yet, I wanted to use this chapter to share some of the crazier stories I've heard. Since I didn't live these myself, it will be hard for me to write them as narratives. Instead, this will read more like a list.

The first comes from Other Author. One night, he delivered, and someone tipped him a puppy.

Another time, Psychologist was delivering pizzas when someone pulled a gun on him. Since Psychologist was already in his car, and he thought the guy was joking, he began to drive. The guy with the gun shot through the hood of the car, lodging a bullet in the battery. Psychologist called the police, and then he called Storyteller. Storyteller—in civilian clothes as he was not working—showed up as the news crews did.

During the newscast, it showed Storyteller while he looked at the damage from the bullet hole. As it showed this, the voiceover read, "detectives at the scene..." Now, Storyteller has a neighbor who thinks that Storyteller is on some undercover job at Pizza Place.

At one point, two of our drivers got in an accident with each other.

Another time, four of our drivers waited at a stoplight in front of the store. A car slammed into the last car in the line. It created a chain reaction, cars piling into each other. All four of our drivers were involved. Though, one specific driver's car took more damage than the others. She required significant repairs to her trunk and rear bumper.

One driver got stuck at an intersection as a highspeed chase ended at that same intersection. She had to step on the pedal and flee to avoid getting caught in what would become a shootout between police and the person who they pursued.

A different driver got stuck in the snow one night. Because he was two blocks away from the store, he decided to walk back to the store and finish his shift. Once we'd clocked out, he walked back to his car, and spent the night in it. The next morning, the snow had melted enough for him to free himself.

One of our female drivers had a guy try to pull her into the door of a hotel room. She yanked her arm away and fled with two guys chasing her. As she reached the front door of the hotel, a second driver from our store happened to arrive on a different delivery. When the people in pursuit saw the second driver, they fled back to their room. By the time the cops arrived, the guys were gone.

Politician is tall and solidly built. He had two smaller men try to mug him. When one would-be mugger reached for him, his reflexes took over. By accident, Politician flung the would-be mugger over a stairway railing, causing the mugger to fall ten feet. The other of the assailants ran.

Once, a driver delivered to a house where a group of five would-be muggers waited for him. He pulled out bear mace and maced them all before continuing to the house. It turned out, the house was vacant. He turned back to the muggers—they were screaming and rubbing their eyes—and he asked them. "So does one of you want to pay for this pizza?"

These are some of the crazier stories my coworkers have gone through, but many of those—and some of mine that I've left out—involve situations that didn't fit the mood of this anthology. They could have been too personal. They might have been too adult. Since I hope all ages can read this book, I've chosen to keep it rated PG.

I want to thank everyone for the time they've taken to read this. I hope you've learned the ins and outs of pizza delivery: laughing, crying, and empathizing with the people in each story. I wanted to be as authentic as I could about the day to day of delivery and to be frank about the oddities drivers come across.

In life, our experience is what defines us, so these stories are personal to me. Some of them have caused me to change as a person. They've helped me regain a love for the people around me, something I had begun to lose while doing eight years of social work.

In closing, I would ask one thing of the reader. The next time you order pizza, understand the risks you're asking of your driver. Recognize the challenges they face, and if they fall short of expectations, don't blame them for it. Maybe they are on the tail end of something crazy that happened to them. The store where they work may be busy. They could be worrying about something happening at home. In the end, they are grateful to have you as a customer, and they want you to be happy. Respect them for that, and please always remember to tip.

Best Wishes,

Josh Walker

Customer Courtesy Checklist

☐ Shovel your sidewalks and driveway.

☐ Warn if there is ice on or near property.

☐ Turn on your porchlight to help the driver find the house quickly and safely.

☐ Keep pets in the other room. They have been known to convince drivers they were the ones who ordered the food.

☐ Dress appropriate.

☐ On Cash deliveries, have money in hand and ready to pay.

☐ Don't make the driver wait for you at the door. On ridiculously hot and insufferably cold days, this applies double.

☐ Be Kind to the driver. If you have a complaint, talk to them with respect and see if they can help. If they can't, they will call the manager to work out a solution.

☐ Always, always, always tip.